Praise for
Stress Management Made Simple

"Dr. Winner offers practical advice for dealing with everyday stress.
You can use this book and CD set to help find **personal peace**
in a chaotic world."
- BRUCE BAGLEY, M.D., PAST PRESIDENT OF THE AMERICAN ACADEMY OF FAMILY PHYSICIANS

"*Stress Management Made Simple* is an extremely important and
effective tool for people dealing with stress and anxiety in our busy world."
*— LYNN MATIS, PSYCHOTHERAPIST SPECIALIZING
IN THE TREATMENT OF ANXIETY*

"*Stress Management Made Simple* is simple, understandable,
and engaging. It is written so that a layman can understand it, but it also
provides physicians with the knowledge and skills they need to help
patients manage stress. This is not material that is taught in medical school
and it's probably not in most residency curricula. I suspect that if more
physicians thought about stress-related disorders in this framework
and utilized the techniques presented in this book we would have
far fewer problems managing stress in our practices."
*— DAVID P. ZAJANO, M.D., CHAIRMAN OF THE DEPARTMENT OF FAMILY
PRACTICE, FRANKLIN SQUARE HOSPITAL, AND FORMER PRESIDENT OF THE
MARYLAND ACADEMY OF FAMILY PRACTICE*

ii | *Stress Management Made Simple*

"The title says it all. Dr. Winner's techniques have enabled County manager
and executives to successfully cope with budget cuts and shifting priorities
while maintaining a collective sanity. **A survival guide**."
— *JOHN J. TORELL, CPA, ESQ.,*
SANTA BARBARA COUNTY ASST AUDITOR-CONTROLLER

"Dr. Winner has an easy, relaxed speaking style with practical stories
to bring home the key concepts. He helps class participants understand
the human body's physiological response to stress and then introduces
stress management skills such as better communication techniques,
breathing exercises, humor, meditation, and re-framing stressful
situations. Every skill is practiced in the book."
— *GAIL WARD, HEALTH EDUCATION SUPERVISOR*

"The Stress Management session you presented to the Santa Barbara County
Education Office management employees at our retreat is deeply appreciated.
Your presentation style was outstanding, conveying your message to the
attendees in a lively style laced with humor and stories that demonstrated your
content. Without exception, the evaluations we received at the end of the day
indicated that the information you presented was enjoyable, helpful and would
be used. Of the evaluations I received a few days after the retreat, every one
indicated that they were already using the relaxation techniques you taught to
the group. You can see that your time with us had great impact."
— *CAROL JOHANSEN, ASSISTANT SUPERINTENDENT,*
SANTA BARBARA COUNTY EDUCATION OFFICE

Stress Management Made Simple

Stress Management Made Simple

JAY WINNER, M.D.

EFFECTIVE WAYS TO BEAT STRESS
FOR BETTER HEALTH

Blue Fountain Press
Santa Barbara, California

Published by

Blue Fountain Press
2026 Cliff Drive, Suite 104
Santa Barbara, CA 93109

ISBN 0-9745119-0-0

Book cover and CD label design by Cole Paciano of Explorium Design

Photography for book cover and CD labels by Mark Weiser

Illustrations by Susan Myers

Portrait photo by Clint Weisman

Interior book design by Michele DeFilippo, 1106 Design

Editing by Donna Beech

*Patient's names and occupations
have been changed to protect their privacy.*

*This book is dedicated to my family,
friends, patients, students
and teachers.*

Contents

Acknowledgements

I owe a debt of gratitude to the following people: First and foremost, I would like to thank my wonderful wife, Dana, who has provided me with love, support, and a lot of excellent advice. My children, Samuel and Zachary, inspire me and continually teach me about life and love.

My mother, Shirley Winner; my late father, Seymour Winner; and my sister, Jody Ginsberg, all helped provide a wonderful, loving environment for me to grow up in and have continued to offer support and love over the years.

I'd like to offer special thanks to my patients and students, who have taught me so much, and thanks to a variety of authors whose wisdom has been made available to me and others.

Cole Paciano of Explorium Design (*www.exploriumdesign.com*) has done an outstanding job designing the book cover and CD labels. His work in creating the *www.stressremedy.com* web site was exceptional. Mark Weiser (*www.photoperception.com*) did the photography for both the cover, CD labels and web site. His numerous superb pictures made it difficult to chose the best for the cover. Don Ollis of A Room With a Vu did an excellent job with the CD recording. Donna Beech did a great job editing the book. Susan Myers' technical drawings really enhanced the book. Michele DeFilippo (*www.1106design.com*) did a superb job with interior book design. Clint Weisman's portrait photography was helpful in the book and for www.stressremedy.com. Thank you to my colleagues at Sansum, my office partner Kari Mathison, M.D., and my excellent office staff. And so many of my friends provided me with invaluable inspiration and help.

I owe a debt of gratitude to the people who reviewed the book for comment. All of these extremely busy people spent their valuable time reviewing the book and CDs. Motivated by their shared vision of helping people deal with stress more effectively, they offered thoughtful suggestions and important comments. They include: Alexander Bystritsky, M.D., Ph.D., Richard Roberts, M.D., J.D., Bruce Bagley, M.D., Laura Richardson Roberts, David Zajano, M.D., Steve Shearer, Ph.D., Larry Bascom, Ph.D., Lynn Matis, M.F.T., Mike Lawson, P.T., M. Greg Stathakis, Nancy Murdock, M.F.T. and Dean Ornish, M.D.

1

Introduction

He who begun has half done.
Dare to be wise, begin.

HORACE

Simply put: **Complete this book and CD set and your ability to manage stress will improve.** After years of teaching stress management to thousands of people, I can make this promise with confidence.

As a family doctor, I have treated everything from acne to heart disease, and from arthritis to depression. Often, the problem was complicated by stress. "The American Academy of Family Physicians estimates that two-thirds of all visits to family doctors are prompted by stress-related symptoms."[1]

Stress is by no means the cause of all medical problems, but there is solid research linking it to a wide variety of physical conditions. One study examined 107 people with heart disease and showed a 74 percent reduction in cardiac events (death, heart attacks and bypass operations) in the group that did stress management training.[2] Another study found that men who had large increases in blood pressure with stress had a 72% increased risk of stroke.[3] Additional ailments associated with stress include: headaches, heartburn, acne, eczema, psoriasis, irritable bowel syndrome, fibromyalgia, depression and infertility. Stress may also affect the treatment of diabetes, high blood pressure, chronic pain, obesity and asthma.

If you are still not convinced about the health effects of stress, consider another study which showed that caregivers under constant stress had a 63% higher chance of dying.[4] Stress affects so many health problems that the *Journal of Occupational and Environmental Medicine* states, "Health-care expenditures are nearly 50% greater for workers who report high levels of stress."[5]

Stress management is part of wholistic health care. Often when someone uses the term wholistic (or holistic medicine), they are referring to alternative medicine. I prefer the definition that describes wholistic as "taking care of the whole person." This is not just important in alternative medicine, but is an essential part of Western medicine. In fact, the core concept of family practice is the "biopsychosocial model;" that is, our degree of health involves a complex interplay between our physical body, our emotions, psychology and social situation (family, friends, work, etc.). The biopsychosocial model is a concept that every first year medical student should know. It is not only well-supported by research; it is also supported by common sense. Our stress levels may affect our headaches. Our headaches may affect our stress levels. Problems involving our social lives may certainly influence our stress levels and our levels of stress can certainly influence our social situations (performance at work, marital health, etc.)

Although doctors are aware that stress influences health, we are often too busy and stressed ourselves to take the time to treat it properly. In many clinics and offices, it is not unusual for a doctor to have 15 minutes to handle three problems, or 30 minutes to do a "complete" history and physical exam. Doctors often see 25 to 35 patients in one day. It is no surprise that doctors frequently recommend fast, but temporary, remedies, instead of more effective treatments requiring lengthy physician-patient discussion. For example, a patient might say, "Doc, my headaches are much worse since I've been so stressed." The doctor's response might be, "Try this medicine next time you get a headache." Alternatively, he/she could say, "Tell me about the stress," and be ready to listen for a while.

Stress can contribute to almost any medical problem. However, stress is not the sole cause of any disease. Medical problems involve a complex interplay of multiple factors, very often including stress. Stress causes real chemical and physical changes in the body. As noted above, cardiac events decreased markedly with stress management. Increased stress causes very real physical changes that can increase the risk of a heart attack. In the same way, if stress contributes to another medical problem, it does not make that problem any less real.

Medications can play an important role in the treatment and prevention of many medical conditions. However, medications usually should be only part of a treatment plan.

Given the time constraints of a typical office visit, what treatment alternatives does the family doctor have? In 1992, I came up with one solution for my medical practice. I organized and led seminars in stress management for my patients and for other doctors' patients. Now, instead of having 15 minutes to handle my patients' complaints about their headache, heartburn and stress, I have six hours to teach stress management skills that can last a lifetime. These patients still have their medicine if they need it, but now there is another option besides a pill that only offers temporary relief.*

Because my first class was so well-received, I scheduled a next one, and then a next. Since 1992, I have taught the classes to thousands of people, including seniors, health professionals, corporate employees, and the general public. Evaluation-form responses have been overwhelmingly positive. Many participants have mentioned the positive impact that the class had on their lives. A number of patients have been unable to attend my classes, but have expressed interest in alternatives to drug therapies for combating stress-related ailments. My goal in writing this book has been to describe the same theories and stress management techniques discussed in my classes in a clear, concise and readable fashion. For some of the techniques, a book format is not sufficient. Therefore, a set of CDs has been included as an integral part of the discussion. In several of the chapters, I suggest that you listen to parts of the CDs in order to gain full benefit from my stress management program. This book and CD combination has become an effective tool for treating my patients.

---

*Note of caution: If a medication has been prescribed to be taken on a regular basis, it is important to discuss the issue with your doctor before discontinuing the medication.

I have tried to make the book neither "gimmicky" nor esoteric. When people are stressed, free time tends to be limited and a 500-page book might be too cumbersome to read. Therefore, the book is concise and to-the-point. I have put a lot of material into a small space, hoping that you will derive maximum benefit for the time you spend. If one of the topics strikes a chord with you, I encourage you to consult the reading list for more extensive study. I have included the points that people who have already taken my classes have said they have found most useful in dealing with stress, as well as a variety of pertinent quotations. The questions of how to deal with stress and how to be happy have been around for thousands of years, and so have some of the best answers.

The first step in our journey will be in defining stress, exploring when stress is a problem and learning a few basic remedies. Following this, we will learn a technique to effectively relax whenever you have few free minutes. This technique, in turn, will form the basis for learning another skill called mindfulness that can very effectively decrease your daily stress.

Next we will explore how small changes in our thoughts can cause large improvements in our ability to handle stress. We will look at how slowing down can help with stress and we will learn ways in which we can put our lives in perspective. Next we investigate basic lifestyle changes that will improve your ability to handle stress. Much of our stress revolves around relationships, so a discussion of communication skills is important. We will learn to manage feelings of anger and frustration, take the stress out of decisions, improve sleep and then learn how to combine a few of the above strategies. Finally in Chapter 14, I'll help you decide if your problems represent more than ordinary stress; and if so, what to do about it.

This book and CD set can be viewed as a stress management tool kit. Depending on your personality and situation, you may find the most value in one or another chapter. If one chapter is not of help, please do not stop reading. You will find other tools in another chapter. I have heard from one reader, "I love this book, and the best part is the first half," and from another reader, "I love this book, and the best part is the second half." Both readers felt that maximum benefit would be gained by completing the entire book and CD set.

You will see that the book draws on a very eclectic mixture of philosophies ranging from Albert Ellis to Carl Rogers to the Dalai Lama to Meyer Friedman and Ray Rosenman to Jon Kabat Zinn, and others. Several of the techniques I created myself for my classes. In order to illustrate concepts throughout the book, I have related a few stories based on my patients and students. Their names and occupations have been changed to ensure their anonymity.

It is important not only to learn stress management techniques, but also to be reminded of principles we already know. I have taught well over a hundred stress management classes. Yet, every time I teach a class, I am reminded of ways to handle my own stress more effectively. In the same way, if you are already familiar with some of the concepts presented in this book, *Stress Management Made Simple* should serve as an important reminder of what may seem like common sense, but is often forgotten.

There is not one ultimate, quick fix for stress. Learning to manage stress well is a life-long pursuit. However, completing this book and CD set is a very healthy start to this endeavor. Some of the initial information might or might not seem basic to you. However, the book chapters and each of the exercises on the CDs build, one upon another. After reading the book and listening to the CDs, you should have a solid introduction to some of the more important aspects of stress management.

You do not have to have severe problems with anxiety to benefit from *Stress Management Made Simple*. My students have ranged from people with minimal stress to people with severe anxiety disorders. Virtually all of them came away with useful information. Everyone has to contend with stress in one way or another. Most people can glean very useful information from this book/CD set. Congratulate yourself for starting the journey to a healthier and happier life. If you make the commitment to finishing the book and following through with the recommendations that make sense to you, your life may never be the same.

---

[1] Hafent, Brent Q., et al. *Mind/Body Medicine: The Effects of Attitudes, Emotions, and Relationships.* Boston: Allyn and Bacon, 1996, p. 48.

[2] Blumenthal, et.al. "Stress Management and Exercise Training in Cardiac Patients With Myocardial Ischemia." *Archives of Internal Medicine.* 1997; 157: 2213–2223.

[3] Everson, Susan, et.al. "Stress-Induced Blood Pressure Reactivity and Incident Stroke in Middle-Aged Men." *Stroke,* 2001; 32: 1263–1270.

[4] Shulz, Richard, Scott Beach. "Caregiving as a Risk Factor for Mortality." *Journal of the American Medical Association.* 1999; 282: 2215–2219.

[5] Sauter, Steven, et al."Stress at Work," National Institute for Occupational Safety and Health (NIOSH), U.S. Department of Health and Human Services. DHH (NIOSH) Pub. No. 99-101. Website: http://www.cdc.gov/niosh/stresswk.html

2

What is Stress?

The process of living is the process of reacting to stress.

STANLEY J. SARNOFF, M.D.

I t is well-documented that our responses to stress directly affect our health. But what exactly is stress? Some aspects of stress can be understood by envisioning the following scenario. Imagine a prehistoric man coming upon a large predator. Out of the corner of his eye, the caveman sees a ferocious saber-tooth tiger. In response, his heart starts pounding faster, his pupils dilate, he starts to sweat, and his blood rushes from his intestines to his muscles. He gets ready to fight the tiger or, if he is a little smarter, to flee from the scene. All of these physiological changes together constitute the caveman's "stress response." Prehistoric men and women who did not have this "fight or flight response" or "stress response" ended up as lunch for the tigers or other predators. Their genes were not passed on.

The fight-or-flight response can still serve to prepare us in times of physical danger. However, in the modern world, the stress response more often occurs when, for example, our bosses yell at us or when we are stuck in traffic. In most of these situations, it is not appropriate to run or fight. Therefore, the stress, in effect, remains in our bodies, and may contribute to illness. To be healthy, we must learn and practice effective ways to deal with stress. Not all stress is bad. It may even serve a purpose at times. However, it is essential to learn to handle stress effectively.

Barbara had high blood pressure and was on four separate medications to lower it. This normally brought her blood pressure down to a normal level of approximately 130 systolic. One evening Barbara mistakenly doubled her evening dose of blood pressure medications. She was terrified that her blood pressure would drop too low, thus endangering her health. She checked her blood pressure several times that night and it averaged 200 systolic. Despite a much higher dose of blood pressure medicine, her blood pressure had very significantly risen, instead of falling. Barbara's fight-or-flight response had had a more potent effect on her blood pressure than all of that medication.

When is Stress a Problem?

As I mentioned earlier, if a tiger charges you, the surge of stress hormones can enable you to run faster. If you are tired, but have an exam to take, a little extra adrenaline may actually improve your test score. We therefore talk of good stress, or "eustress." Eustress can improve performance and can be often felt as excitement, passion and enthusiasm.

However, if your stress level increases beyond a certain point, your performance will decline. Stress is a problem when it is either very elevated or very prolonged. This bad stress is called "distress" and, in the long run, it can contribute to some of the medical problems listed in Chapter One. One way to recognize distress is that it just plain feels bad. Signs of distress can include: feelings of anxiety or worry, muscular tension, fatigue, heart racing, insomnia, irritability, shakiness, excessive sweating, upset stomach or a sense of being overwhelmed.

If you are having any of these problems, this is the book for you. If you are having any of the medical problems worsened by stress, this book will likely improve your health.

Stress management techniques can be grouped into two broad categories: external changes we can make in our lives, and internal changes we can make by modifying our thought processes.

External Changes

Even if you're on the right track, you'll get run over if you just sit there.
WILL ROGERS

If you have a size 9 foot, but are wearing size 6 shoes and your feet hurt, don't just sit there and try to bear it — get new shoes! Sometimes the best action we can take to manage stress is to change our environments. It might not be easy, but if your spouse beats you, it may be best to find a shelter and move out. If there is a better job down the street, perhaps you should quit your current one. Sometimes the need to make external change is obvious, but not always.

For example, I know a nurse who earned a promotion. It seemed like a good opportunity — better pay and more prestige as the head of a department. But, during the two years she spent at the new job, she found herself becoming increasingly stressed and unhappy. With some further thought, she realized that the additional administrative responsibilities in her new job were keeping her from spending time with patients. Patient care was the part of nursing she really enjoyed. Returning to her old job was her most effective stress management technique.

External changes are not just limited to quitting a job or moving to a new town. The best change may be to stay at the same job, but to delegate, modify, or eliminate certain tasks. Frequently, people get stuck in inefficient practices. Being open to change is essential in managing stress and in doing well in your business and personal life.

Another type of external strategy is to reasonably prepare for the future. Examples would be: 1. working out finances for your basic needs, children's education and retirement; 2. keeping adequate insurance for you and your family; 3. discussing family emergency plans (e.g., for fires, earthquakes or hurricanes, depending on where you live); 4. using your seat belt and driving carefully; 5. wearing a bicycle helmet when you're bicycling.

Making external changes is a key strategy for managing stress. Stress can be a wake up call — a signal to set new goals in your life. What are your dreams? Creating personal, financial and spiritual goals, and making plans to meet those goals are important. These goals and plans will help you manage your stress and help you achieve a full and exciting life. Take a moment now to think about what you would like improved in your life. What can you do to reach these goals and perhaps decrease the stress in your life? If you are not sure whether a particular change is the best choice, read the rest of the book and look for alternative ways of managing your stress, then reexamine the question.

Carol had terrible migraine headaches and severe muscle pain from fibromyalgia. She had tried a variety of medications and other treatments with only partial success. Carol began to confide in me that she was thinking about leaving a relationship. It turned out that her boyfriend of several years was alcoholic. He would not consider quitting alcohol. Carol was in individual counseling and also was going to Alanon. Her boyfriend would not consider either individual or couples counseling. Carol was getting tired of "sleeping with someone every night that smelled of alcohol" and she was tired of never knowing when her boyfriend would "explode." Her headaches would often occur after arguments with her boyfriend, and, interestingly, she described the sensation as her head "exploding," as well. Then she took a two-week vacation with her family, away from her boyfriend. She did not have one headache during those two weeks. She later realized that her relationship was not healthy for her. Her improved health continued when she got out of the unhealthy relationship. (This story actually combines elements of two patients' stories.)

Internal Changes

The last of the human freedoms — to choose one's attitude
in any given set of circumstances, to choose one's own way.
VICTOR FRANKEL

An external or environmental change is not always the best solution. If we look for the jobs that always meets all of our desires, we will undoubtedly be frustrated. If we insist that our friends, spouses, or children always meet our standard of "perfection," we will be disappointed. We may adequately prepare for the future and still be overwhelmed by stress. To handle stress well, not only do we need to know when to alter our environment, but also when to use internally based techniques.

Even minor changes in a person's internal response can dramatically influence the way that a person deals with stress. Some people thrive in what others would consider very stressful jobs (e.g., brain surgeons or police officers), while others have overwhelming amounts of distress in seemingly less stressful jobs.

In addition to changing our external circumstances, there is much we can do internally to influence our level of distress. Often all that is needed is a change in perspective or a little practice in stress coping techniques. In the rest of the book we will work together to explore these strategies.

3

ᨀᨀᨀ

Learn to Relax

Relaxing is like playing an instrument. To become proficient
we must practice, practice, practice.

PIERRE

The first step in learning to relax during a normal day is learning to
relax for a specified period of time. In the last chapter we discussed
the stress response. Now let's consider the opposite, or what Herbert
Benson, M.D. calls the "relaxation response."[7] Benson based his relaxation
response on a technique thousands of years old called meditation.

If you have any preconceived ideas about meditation, please put them
aside. Meditation is a simple relaxation technique — and more. By learning this technique, you will learn skills that can be applied during a normal day — making your days much less stressful and much more enjoyable.

---

*Sarah was experiencing leg cramps one evening and decided
to listen to the meditation on Track 1 of the first CD. By the
time the meditation was over, her leg pain was gone.*

*Similarly, Bob was having a headache when he started
listening to the CD. His headache was 50 percent better by
the end of the meditation.*

Beth was 78 years old and was very concerned about how she would tolerate a one-hour dental procedure. She decided that the dental chair would be an ideal spot to practice her meditation. Before she knew it, the procedure was over and the dentist was amazed at how well Beth had done.

Amy was a 39-year-old physical therapist when she first saw me. Her blood pressure was very elevated and she was having trouble coping with her work-related stress. I discussed the fact that her treatment would likely include blood pressure medication, but first, I recommended that she address her diet, exercise, and stress management. She started meditating daily and working on the mindfulness techniques described in the next chapter. When I saw her at our next visit two weeks later, her blood pressure was normal without medication, and she was coping with work much better. *

The first step in learning meditation is to learn *diaphragmatic breathing*. The diaphragm is a large dome-shaped muscle that separates the chest from the abdomen. As you breathe in, the diaphragm contracts and flattens out. The lungs fill the lower chest cavity and the abdomen expands (see, Figure 1). When people are anxious, they tend to breathe without using the diaphragm and, instead, use the muscles in the neck and chest. Anxious people also tend to breathe quickly or hyperventilate. Among other effects, the hyperventilation temporarily alters the acid-base balance of the blood, thereby increasing the feelings of anxiety.

One of the benefits of diaphragmatic breathing is that it is much more relaxing. Sometimes a few nice, deep breaths are all you need to be

---

* **Note of caution:** It is very important to get regular screenings for high blood pressure and not to stop blood pressure medication without a doctor's supervision. Untreated high blood pressure is associated with a significantly higher risk of stroke and heart attack. Although some studies have shown a reduction of blood pressure from regular meditation, many people still require medication.

calmer. Breathe in through your nose, and let your abdomen gently move outward with each inhalation. As you initially learn diaphragmatic breathing, it may be helpful to put one hand on your abdomen. Let your hand rise with each breath in. You may breathe out through your nose or mouth. If you have trouble getting comfortable with this style of breathing, try breathing while lying flat on your back. Diaphragmatic breathing is both an important component of meditation and a relaxation exercise in its own right.

If you are still having trouble getting the hang of diaphragmatic breathing, do not get frustrated. Be patient and give yourself time to get used to it. When I was in college, an exercise physiologist performed free posture evaluations as part of a research study. I was advised to stand with my shoulders further back. Initially, it seemed very strange and awkward. However, within a few weeks, my improved posture felt natural. Similarly, as you practice the diaphragmatic breathing, it will become more natural.

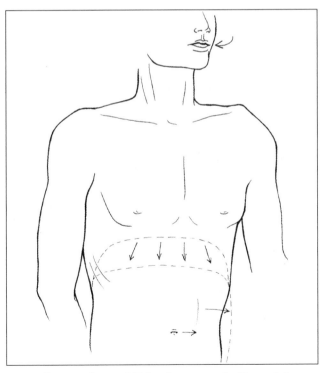

Illustration of Diaphragmatic Breathing

Tom is a busy corporate executive who came to me complaining of coughing fits that had been going on for over a month. He would have four or five of the "fits" per day. The fits would start as a tickle in his throat, then he would start coughing, and feel like he could not get a full breath. When he was in an important business meeting, he would start to worry about having a coughing fit, and invariably, he would start coughing. A previous doctor had prescribed antibiotics, but the fits persisted.

As we were discussing the various options to treat his problem, Tom started getting a "tickle" in his throat. However, this time he focused on slow, diaphragmatic breaths and he didn't get the coughing fit that usually followed. Tom ended up not needing the prescription medicine we had considered trying.

Jim was in his 50s and had a long history of Parkinson's Disease. To add to his challenges, he had developed heart disease and, later, a rare tumor of his stomach, called a carcinoid. He required a major surgery to remove the tumor and part of his stomach.

As he was coming out of the anesthesia, he realized that he had missed his Parkinson's Disease medication. His body was feeling stiff and he was losing control of his muscles. He was becoming very anxious. His heart was racing, more and more. He was starting to feel short of breath. Then he remembered what he had learned in my stress management class. Although he was uncomfortable, he focused on diaphragmatic breathing and his heart rate dropped. He was no longer short of breath and he started feeling much better.

Once you learn diaphragmatic breathing, you are ready to move on and learn meditation. It is best to be comfortable as you practice meditation.

Try to wear loose, comfortable clothing that does not constrict your chest or waist, and find a comfortable place to sit down. Begin your meditation when you are not excessively hungry, thirsty or full. Meditation may be done while sitting up straight in a chair with your arms and legs uncrossed, while sitting on a pillow on the floor, or while lying down. On Track 1 of the first CD, I will guide you in learning to meditate. I will ask you to focus primarily on your breath as it flows in and out. As you listen, remember to use diaphragmatic breathing.

As you meditate, you will probably have many thoughts. This is normal. The goal with meditation is to practice rapidly letting each thought go as soon as you notice it, and then returning your focus back on your breath. With practice, this will become easier to do. By mastering the ability to observe your thoughts in a nonjudgmental fashion, and let them go, you will be well on your way to coping effectively with many stressful situations.*

After finishing this paragraph, it would be an ideal time to find a comfortable place to listen to Track 1 of the first CD. **Never listen to the CD while driving or while operating potentially dangerous machinery.** If you are pressed for time, it may be helpful to know that you can finish Meditation 1 in about 16 minutes. There are approximately 16 minutes of guided meditation, followed by 24 minutes of silence, occasionally interrupted by the sound of a bell. The bells serve two purposes. An individual bell ring serves as a reminder to return to noticing your breath. A series of three bells alerts you that you have been meditating for 20, 30 and then 40 minutes, successively. If you just cannot put the book down long enough now to do the above meditation, either do the six minute meditation on Track 2 of CD 3 or you may skip ahead to reading Chapter 5. (However, if you skip Chapters 3 and 4, be sure to come back to what most feel is the most important, life-changing part of the book/CD set.)

This meditation may be used repeatedly. After a few sessions, you may decide to meditate without the CD. When you are very pressed for time, you may use the six minute meditation on CD 2, Track 3.

---

*During the guided meditation, you will be asked to avoid resisting body sensations. Although serious medical problems (such as heart problems) are less likely during relaxation, they can occur at any time. Therefore, never ignore any severe pain, chest pain, or significant breathing problems.

Reading about meditation may seem a little dry to some people. However, by the end of the Chapter 4, you will see how meditation provides a foundation for learning to deal with stress throughout the day.

1. View your meditation sessions as a reward, as time you set aside for yourself — not as another chore or task to complete.

2. When you learn to meditate, it is ideal to be in a comfortable setting. It is best to learn in quiet surroundings. Later, you might enjoy the challenge of a noisier setting. You can let any noise be a signal for you to go deeper into your meditation.

3. Positions suitable for meditation include: sitting in a chair with your legs uncrossed and hands flat on your lap, sitting on a pillow on the floor, or lying on your back. One disadvantage — or perhaps, advantage — of meditating lying down is that you may fall asleep during the meditation. This might be an advantage, if it is time to go to bed, but it might be a disadvantage if it is a workday morning and you do not hit the snooze button on the alarm.

4. Start with diaphragmatic breathing and pay keen attention to your breath as it enters your nostrils, throat, lungs, and abdomen.

5. When thoughts come to mind, do not resist them. Instead of judging the thoughts, just notice them, and then gently let them go. Imagine each thought as a cloud floating by, or a branch floating down a stream. Do not be discouraged if you have an abundance of thoughts. Meditation is not about having zero thoughts, but rather about developing your ability to gently let the thoughts go as soon as they appear. After letting each thought go, pay full attention to, and enjoy your very next breath. Consider that each thought you have provides you more practice in the skill of quickly letting thoughts go. Don't be surprised if your meditation sessions initially consist of a lot of thinking and only a few minutes focused on the breath. A transcript of your thoughts during a meditation might read: "... I have a bunch of dishes to do. I also need to get a lot of work done tomorrow — oh yeah, I'm meditating .... I wonder what time ... My back ..." Don't worry; as long as you learn to gently let the thoughts go and focus back on the next breath, the meditation is working.

6. Avoid resisting your body sensations. Sometimes, the more you resist an uncomfortable sensation, the more spasm you create in the surrounding area. When you stop resisting the sensation, sometimes the discomfort eases.

7. You might try a body scan toward the beginning of the meditation. Relax one body part of your body at a time, starting either with your feet or head.

8. Another alternative to focusing on your breath is to focus on a repetitive phrase called a *mantra*. Thich Nhat Hahn, a renowned meditation teacher, suggests repeating the following statements to yourself, "Breathing in, I calm my body. Breathing out, I smile," and with the next breath, "Dwelling in the present moment" (as you inhale), "I know this is a wonderful moment" (as you exhale). To shorten the phrases you can try "calm — smile; present moment — wonderful moment."[8] Hahn also recommends meditating with a half smile on your face. Herbert Benson, M.D., a prominent mind-body researcher, believes that people with a religious tradition may gain additional benefit from repeating a short prayer as a mantra. He believes that repetition of the short prayer phrase lets the mind and body remember additional feelings of wellness.[9] Other potential mantras include: "one," "love," "peace," "relax," or any other phrase that you find relaxing and/or meaningful. You may experiment to find a phrase or phrases which work best for you.

9. Generally, it is best to continue the meditation session uninterrupted. If you occasionally have very important thoughts, you can keep a notepad and pencil by you. If you decide to do this, however, you should use the notepad rarely. The notepad becomes useful if otherwise you would be spending 20 minutes worried about forgetting, or actually forgetting, an important responsibility (such as picking someone up at the airport).

10. I would recommend starting your meditation practice with your eyes closed. Later, you can try meditating with your eyes open. This can be done by maintaining an unfocused gaze or by focusing on an object, such as a flower or a candle.

11. If you'd like, you may end the meditation with a phrase; such as, giving thanks for the present moment, the people in your life, your health, etc.

12. Like exercise, meditation can be used on an as-needed basis. However, there is much benefit to incorporating meditation into your daily routine. Perhaps, instead of hitting the snooze button several times, you might sit up in bed, when the alarm goes off, and do a meditation to start your day. Alternatively, right after work or before dinner may be a good time for you.

13. There are different opinions about how long to meditate. For instance, when people begin learning "Transcendental Meditation" or "TM," they are usually asked to meditate for 20 minutes, twice a day. At the University of Massachusetts Stress Management Course, Jon Kabat-Zinn, Ph.D. starts people in his seminar with the obligation of meditating 40 minutes a day. There is no perfect amount of time to meditate. In fact, it would be an interesting research study to see how people benefit from different meditation schedules. I suggest that you meditate at least 10 minutes a day and, on occasion, meditate at least few minutes after you have the thought, "I feel like stopping." It is nice to realize that you do not have to respond to a thought as soon as you have it and, instead, can enjoy a few more minutes of meditation.

14. Like many things, meditation takes practice and dedication. Do not expect one meditation session to be like another. It is helpful to continue your regular practice despite any thoughts of boredom or discontent. There is a great deal to be learned from meditating when your mind is distracted. Learning to deal with distracting thoughts in meditation will teach you important skills that can be used throughout the day.

---

[7] Benson, Herbert, M.D. and Miriam Z. Klipper, *The Relaxation Response.* Harper Torch. 2000 (initial version in 1975)

[8] Hanh, Thich Nhat, *Present Moment Wonderful Moment.* Berkeley, CA, 1990, p.32.

[9] Benson, Herbert and Marg Stark, *Timeless Healing,* New York: Fireside, 1997.

4

Learn to Enjoy Your Day

In order to be utterly happy, the only thing necessary is to refrain from comparing this moment with other moments in the past, which I often did not fully enjoy because I was comparing them with other moments of the future.

ANDRE GIDE

I can feel guilty about the past, apprehensive about the future, but only in the present can I act. The ability to be in the present moment is a major component of mental wellness.

ABRAHAM MASLOW

The secret of health for both mind and body is not to mourn for the past, not to worry about the future, nor to anticipate troubles, but to live the present moment wisely and earnestly.

BUDDHA

Enjoyable, healthy activities, such as hiking, bathing, eating, watching a sunset, or listening to music are good for you and can reduce your stress level. However, if you obsess about your problems as you participate in these activities, the benefit will be minimal. Eating a healthy gourmet meal can help reduce stress, but only if you taste the food, rather than spend the time worrying about problems at work. Playing tennis can be a relaxing activity, but not if you spend most of the game angry at yourself for not playing well.

The purpose of this chapter is to help you make your relaxing activities truly relaxing and your stressful activities less stressful and more enjoyable. An extremely effective method of decreasing stress and increasing enjoyment is the practice of mindfulness. Mindfulness is a practice that has evolved over thousands of years and, because of its effectiveness, it is a cornerstone of this book.

The Present Moment

Mindfulness involves focusing your attention on the present moment. To begin exploring the concept of mindfulness, consider the question: "How many ways can the present be — not tomorrow, not five minutes from now, not even one second from now, but this very moment?" The present moment can only be one way. In other words, the present moment can only be as it is. In five seconds we may be able to effect a change, but *right now* can only exist the way it is.

Nevertheless, the average person spends a tremendous amount of time wishing that the present moment were different. As soon as the alarm goes off in the morning, a stream of thoughts begin: " I don't feel like waking up now .... I wish I didn't have to go to work .... if only it weren't so cold and rainy out .... I wish the kids would be quieter .... if only my spouse (boss or friend) would act differently .... I wish my back would feel better .... I feel overwhelmed" and so on. What a stressful way to begin the day! It is a useful exercise to start paying attention to how much time during your day is spent wishing that the present moment were different.

Applying Mindfulness

By applying the mindfulness skills learned in meditation, a potentially aggravating situation can be turned into a more pleasant experience. For instance, let's say you are stressed while in a traffic jam. When you think about it, a traffic jam should be a low stress experience. There are not a lot of decisions to make. All we usually need to do is follow the car in front of us. Why is it stressful? Most likely we are saying or thinking something to the effect of: "I wish I weren't here .... What bad luck I have .... Those other drivers are idiots ..... I can't be late...." In other words, we wish the present moment were different.

Instead of spending the next 30 minutes stressed out, take what you learned in your meditation and use it. Don't get angry at the negative thoughts; they are a normal response. When you notice the thoughts, gently let them go and notice your next breath. Perhaps those thoughts will come up again and again. Each time a thought arises, you can gently let it go in the same nonjudgmental fashion. Do not worry if a particular negative thought occurs frequently. The skill lies in seeing how quickly you can let the thought go, so that you can enjoy the present moment just as it is. Similar to the meditation practice, each thought gives you an additional opportunity to practice the skill of letting thoughts go gently and quickly.

Importance of Thoughts and Goals

Mindfulness practice is not meant to discourage thought. Without our thoughts we would not know how to tie our shoes, much less how to build computers or cure life-threatening diseases. However, a key to managing stress and enjoying life is learning how to let certain nonproductive thoughts go, enabling yourself to enjoy the present moment.

Practicing mindfulness does not mean our goals should be abandoned. Without goals, we would accomplish very little. We can and should work to make changes in the future, but in doing so, we should also challenge ourselves to enjoy the process. Reinhold Niebuhr said, in the often-quoted serenity prayer: "Oh God, give us serenity to accept what cannot be changed; courage to change what should be changed; and wisdom to distinguish the one from the other." I would add, "Please give us the knowledge that change often takes time and the wisdom to enjoy the process of change." In other words, we should use mindfulness as a tool to enjoy the journey. Without mindfulness, life can become a never-ending series of desires, with little enjoyment of the here-and-now. While in high school, we can't wait to graduate and enter college. As a college student, you want to graduate and start working. When working, we might wish for retirement. Maybe we think that life will be better if we are married; or if we're married, we think that divorce will bring us happiness. If happiness were achieved only when our goals were met, our happiness will be short lived indeed, since another "need" is always around the corner.

> For a long time it had seemed to me that life was about to begin — real life. But there was always some obstacle in the way, something to be got through first, some unfinished business, time still to be served, a debt to be paid. Then life would begin. At last it dawned on me that these obstacles were my life.
> ALFRED D' SOUZA

Mindfulness and Stress

Even a small increase in the amount of mindfulness can dramatically improve the way that you handle stress in your life. Figure 2 illustrates what occurs when the stress is really a problem. As successive stressful events occur, they act in a cumulative fashion and result in an elevated level of stress. When this high level of stress is sustained for long periods of time, both physical and emotional problems are likely to arise. In contrast, each time you bring yourself to enjoy the present moment, even for a short period of time, it decreases your level of stress (see, Figure 3). An increase in mindfulness from one percent to two percent of your day may not seem like much. However, as you can see from Figure 3, it doubles your stress reduction.

The Stress Cycle

Sometimes people elevate their anxiety level by trying to resist their anxious feelings. In other words, they get anxious about being anxious. The following example illustrates this type of nonproductive cycle.

FIGURE 2

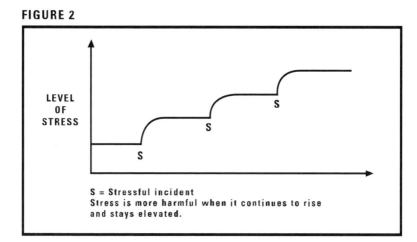

S = Stressful incident
Stress is more harmful when it continues to rise
and stays elevated.

FIGURE 3

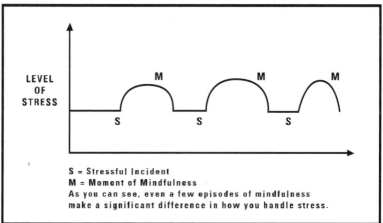

S = Stressful Incident
M = Moment of Mindfulness
As you can see, even a few episodes of mindfulness
make a significant difference in how you handle stress.

If your heart is pounding fast and you don't like the feeling, you might resist the sensation and wish your heart would slow down (Figure 4, arrow 1). However, the more you resist the sensation, the faster your heart pounds and the worse you feel (Figure 4, arrow 2). In addition to this cycle, another cycle may contribute to the anxiety. For instance, you might blame the anxiety on your supervisor's actions. If you focus your thoughts on wishing that your boss behaved differently, you end up resisting the present circumstance (Figure 4, arrow 3). Your heart rate and anxiety then further increase (Figure 4, arrow 4).

Some people attempt to relieve stress by engaging in an automatic behavior or habit, such as smoking, nail biting, or overeating (Figure 4, arrow 5). These habits are largely nonproductive and may be harmful in the long run.

FIGURE 4

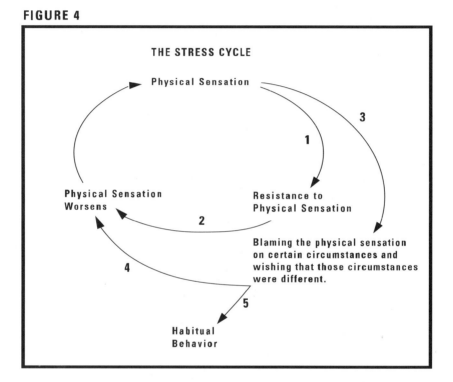

THE STRESS CYCLE

Let's look at another way of handling the situation. When a patient comes to me complaining of a racing heart, I start by asking enough questions to reassure both of us that the sensation is not caused by a medical problem.* If the racing heart is caused by anxiety, as it most frequently is, I sometimes tell my patient to let his or her heart beat as fast as it can. That's right — I instruct the person to sit down, take some diaphragmatic breaths, and let his or her heart beat as fast as it likes. This technique often slows the racing heart and decreases the anxiety

---

*See, Chapter 14, page 138 for information on evaluating palpitations (the sensation of a prominent, fast or irregular heartbeat).

because it breaks the vicious cycle described in Figure 4. The person is no longer resisting the physical sensation.

Similarly, making a conscious effort not to resist external circumstances, such as your supervisor's behavior, can also decrease your stress level. Perhaps you can change his/her future behavior with some tactful feedback. However, for the present moment, focusing on the wish that your boss were different is counterproductive.

If you notice yourself engaging in an automatic behavior or habit, pay attention to the physical sensations and thoughts that tend to occur prior to performing the behavior. Let the associated thoughts go as you focus on your breath. Rather than "running away" from the uncomfortable physical sensations by grabbing a cigarette or habitually turning on the television, try to sit with the feeling for a few moments. By accepting the knot in your stomach, and taking some mindful diaphragmatic breaths, you may find that the discomfort decreases or passes altogether. By resisting a sensation, we often make it worse than it would otherwise be.

It is ideal to break the cycle described in Figure 4 as soon as it starts. Don't spend 20 minutes wishing things were different. *As soon as you notice a "resistant thought," let the thought go and focus back on the next breath.* As with meditation, if the thought comes up again, patiently let it go again. Remember that the more thoughts you have, the more practice you gain in letting the thoughts go. Also, as with meditation, remember to breathe using your diaphragm. By learning to recognize the thoughts and feelings of stress early, you can break the stress cycle before it starts, or at least before it goes very far.

Pay attention to your body. Do you tend to tense certain muscle groups when under stress? Typical muscle groups that tense in the stress response include the neck, shoulders, back, abdomen, hands, jaw, and face (especially the little muscles between the eyes). If you typically tense your shoulders as you get stressed, learn to focus on your shoulders as soon as you notice the stress. As you focus on your shoulders, allow them to relax just as you did with the meditation during the first meditation on CD 1. The muscle relaxation is easiest when you do it early in the stress response.

Take a moment now to list the muscle groups that tend to tense the most when you are stressed:

1. _____

2. _____

3. _____

4. _____

If you do not know the answer now, pay attention to your body when you are stressed and then fill in the list.

In summary, when you find yourself stressed and wishing the present moment to be different, simply let the thought go, focus on a diaphragmatic breath, and perhaps relax a muscle group.

Sam was 17 years old when he came to see me. He was having recurrent headaches and nausea. He hated taking medications and wanted to explore other treatment options. Sam experienced stress about several different issues in his life, such as his high school basketball games. Typically, he would feel a little nervous, wish he felt differently, and start clenching his jaw. Soon his headache would begin. After we talked, Sam tried another approach. As soon as he felt himself starting to get stressed or wishing he felt differently, he would let the thoughts go, focus on diaphragmatic breathing, and relax his jaw. By the time of our next visit, Sam's headaches were occurring much less frequently.

Eustress

Adopting the right attitude can convert a negative stress into a positive one.
HANS SELYE

Many people like roller coasters, but few enjoy the beginning of the ride. Your palms get sweaty, your heart pounds, and your pupils dilate. When you reach the top of the roller coaster and look down that first big hill, you're convinced you're going to die! As the ride continues, you find yourself excited and enjoying the swift turns. Wait a minute — what happened? Your heart is still pounding fast, your palms are still sweaty, and your pupils are still dilated, but now you're having fun. What's different?

At the beginning of the ride, maybe you were wishing that you were somewhere else and that your body would feel differently, (e.g., your palms would not be as sweaty). Toward the middle and end of the ride, you just enjoyed the ride for what it was. In other words, as you stopped resisting the experience, the anxiety was transformed into excitement.

In Chapter 2, I discussed that all stress is not bad. There is bad stress called "distress" and good stress called "eustress." Now say the word eustress slowly out loud. *"Eustress" sounds a lot like "use stress," doesn't it?* How many performers have gotten up in front of thousands of people and never had a surge of adrenaline? Probably not many. The good ones learn to use that excess energy. *At times, it is best to handle stress by using the additional energy to be excited and to enthusiastically pursue your goals.*

Although not all stress is bad, the statement,"I'm stressed," has a very negative connotation to most people. Just the thought of being stressed can lead us to resist our feelings. In turn, the more we resist stress, the more distressed we get. In a sense, we get anxious about being anxious. Solution? Try replacing the thoughts, "I'm stressed, " or "I'm stressed out," with the thoughts "I have a high energy level," or "My adrenaline level is up," and then go use that energy. By reframing the situation in this way, you can let yourself enjoy how your body feels in the moment, as opposed to resisting the sensations. Sometimes you might lessen stress by listening to mellow music. Other times, you might manage stress by singing and dancing to an upbeat tune.

Enjoying the Present

The purpose of life is to live it, to taste experience to the utmost,
to reach out eagerly and without fear for richer and newer experience.
ELEANOR ROOSEVELT

To further explore mindfulness, consider how your mind works when you are feeling your best. Most people can recall moments of peak experience, such as gazing into a lover's eyes, holding their newborn child, walking on the beach during a sunset, standing on a surfboard for the first time, or skiing in deep powder. They may try to return to the same beach or hiking trail and try to reproduce the peak experience. Frequently, the second experience does not live up to their memories of the initial experience. All peak experiences share a common element. They occur when you are fully present, enjoying the moment just as it is, as opposed to wishing this or that were different. During a peak experience of enjoying a magnificent sunset, we are not thinking to ourselves: "If only the sunset had a little more pink, instead of the orange, then it would be OK." Rather, we enjoy the sunset just as it is in the present moment.

The mindfulness that spontaneously helps us appreciate a peak experience can also help us find joy in simple activities. Taking a shower, eating, driving, walking, or even doing the dishes, can become a relaxation exercise. When we wash dishes, we are often thinking about how we would like to be done already. Thich Nhat Hahn does a dish washing meditation instead: he fills the sink and enjoys the feeling of his hands in the warm sudsy water — enjoying washing one dish at a time.[10]

The opportunities to enjoy the present moment are limitless. We can enjoy the next breath, the next step, the warm water in the shower, the cold water in the pool, or many different aromas from the smell of dinner to the smell of a flower. Instead of being totally distracted when we eat or comparing our current meal to another, we can take a few seconds to smell the aroma, to look at the food, to notice the texture and how it feels in different parts of our mouths.

During one session of my stress management class, we do a meditation in which we very slowly savor one strawberry for about 10 minutes. We appreciate the unique appearance of the strawberry and enjoy its fragrance, texture and taste. A classic type of meditation is the walking meditation. Next time you walk from one office to the next, instead of worrying about your work, notice each breath and notice the ground massaging your feet with every step. As you notice each breath and let your thoughts go, you'll start noticing that what at first appeared to be boring, everyday scenery is actually worthy of a postcard.

Turn everyday routines into special moments of relaxation. Make a bath or shower into a meditation — feel the warm water on your body, enjoy your fingers massaging your scalp as you shampoo, notice the soap lather, and feel the texture of the towel as you dry off. Even as you brush your teeth, you can notice the bristles of the brush massaging your gums. As you pet your dog or cat, pay attention to how the fur feels on your fingers and hands. Notice the scenery to enjoy your trip to work. Do some mindful stretching (on your own or in a yoga class). Notice the sounds of the birds or crickets. Be mindful as you make love to your lover. Any practice of mindfulness has the opportunity to spill over to the other areas of your life. Immerse yourself in music, feel the warm sun, the brisk refreshing cold or a soothing breeze on your face ....

Reminders of Mindfulness

We have discussed how mindfulness is as simple as enjoying your next breath or feeling the ground massage your foot as you step. We have also discussed that increasing the frequency of these mindful episodes is a key to managing stress. What strategies, then, can we employ to increase the frequency of mindfulness? Consider using both of these methods:

1. As soon as you notice stress or a thought wishing the present to be different, develop the reflex of letting the thought go and focusing on the present breath, footstep, etc. (Also, consider relaxing a muscle group that you tend to tense under times of stress.)

2.   Assign certain events to be reminders to breathe mindfully.

In *Peace is Every Step,* Thich Nhat Hanh describes his experiences at a Buddhist monastery.[11] Periodically throughout the day, a bell would ring. The sound of the bell was a signal to let any thoughts go and to enjoy the next breath. Now, when he hears a telephone ring, he uses that sound as a reminder to enjoy the next breath instead of answering the phone immediately. Many occurrences can be used as reminders to enjoy the present moment. Next time you are driving, decide that each red light will be a reminder to enjoy the next breath.[12] For most people, a ringing telephone or red light are not reminders of mindfulness. However, in order to increase mindful times throughout the day, we can consciously assign these events to be such reminders.

The sound of the beeper can be another reminder to breathe mindfully. Seeing the brake lights of the car in front of you could be a reminder. Another reminder might be a picture or a saying on the wall.

On my office wall, I had a picture with the caption: "Success is a journey, not a destination." Different quotations may have a special way of speaking to you. I just ordered some coffee mugs with the saying: "Take a little quiet time every day." As I drink my tea, I will see another reminder.

The reminder to enjoy the present moment may involve a daily routine. When a doctor looks at the next patient's chart, it can be a signal to notice the next breath. As health care workers wash their hands between patients, it can be a useful reminder to feel the soap and water, and notice the fragrance of the hand lotion they might put on afterwards. Having dishes to do can be a reminder to do a dish washing meditation.

Sounds that are normally irritating can become reminders. If you are the parent of a baby, decide that each time the baby starts crying, it will be a reminder for you. It will be a signal to let go of thoughts wishing the present moment were different, to focus on your diaphragmatic breaths, and to relax a muscle group, as you attend to your child's needs. (You might doubt this can work. However, if people use breathing exercises to deal with several types of pain — including the pain of childbirth — it can work in circumstances such as this as well.)

One of my patients made regular trips to the Xerox machine as part of her work. This was her reminder. During work, another patient used Microsoft Outlook in order to schedule several times a day where a pop up window on her computer would say "breathe." She would then take a 5-minute break to focus on her breath. The morning alarm clock, intermittent watch alarm, or bell of a larger clock can also be signals to let go of thoughts and to focus on the next breath. Another one of my class members took the stress management class with a coworker. Throughout the day they would just remind each other to breathe.

Many of us in the medical field enjoy seeing patients, but dread paperwork and dictation. The small annoyance of a single dictation may not be a big deal, but if it happens 10 or 20 times a day, the frustration builds. Complete medical records are important for thorough patient care. If instead of complaining, we would take that opportunity to enjoy a mindful breath, there would be 10 or 20 times that day that the stress can be decreased instead of increased. Every instance adds up.

Just reading through this section quickly may have minimal impact on your life. To make this technique more meaningful for you, take some time now to assign commonplace or everyday events to be reminders for you to take some mindful diaphragmatic breaths. Feel free to include the reminders mentioned above, and see if you can think of some additional ones. Refer to the list on a regular basis to help ingrain the reminders into your mind. If several mornings in a row, you read a list that includes "car brake lights," you will soon think of mindful breathing as soon as you notice the brake lights of the car in front.

Right now write some reminders and add new reminders when you think of them. Think of a couple of reminders to be used during work and some for home and other activities.

1. _____

2. _____

3. _____

4. _____

5. _____

6. _____

7. _____

8. _____

9. _____

10. _____

Let's say you've chosen at least three reminders of mindfulness and that one of those things is red traffic lights. You review the reminders a few times and, later in the day, you actually see a red light as you are driving, but a wave of peacefulness does not spontaneously descend upon you from heaven. So, you immediately conclude, "This stuff doesn't work!"

Well, you were pretty close, but missed the point by a hair. Being reminded is the beginning, not the end. When you see the red light, you must deliberately let any thoughts go and focus on taking a diaphragmatic breath. (Optionally, you can relax one of the muscle groups that you typically tense.)

Worrying About the Future

Another source of stress is worrying about the future. Here, mindfulness can also be beneficial. We should take precautions for safety and security. If you are worried about your future health, appropriate precautions would include: quitting smoking, installing and maintaining working fire alarms at home, and wearing your seat belt when you are in a car. Other safety precautions for the future would include obtaining appropriate insurance and wise financial planning.

Let's say that you have taken these reasonable precautions (or you are working on them to the best of your ability), yet you still are preoccupied with worries of the future. These worries can be dealt with in the same mindful fashion that we have previously discussed. Quickly and repeatedly, let each thought go and focus back on the diaphragmatic breath, muscle relaxation and/or another present-moment sensation.

"It's Too Hard" and "I'm Overwhelmed" are Just Thoughts

As people start exploring mindfulness, they sometimes think, "This is too hard," or "I can't do it." These ideas are nothing but thoughts to notice and let go; then you can enjoy the next breath. It may be impossible to be mindful every moment of the next year, or even the next hour or next minute. However, it is easy to enjoy that very next breath, just like you did in the meditation. If you have the thought that you need "peace of mind" or a "clear mind" before you can relax, remind yourself that those are just abstract concepts. All you need to do is let these thoughts go and enjoy the very next breath. Remember, even if you increase the amount of mindfulness in your life by a small amount, your overall stress level can markedly impove.

Most of us have had the thought "I'm overwhelmed" at one time or another. Mindfulness teaches us to let that thought go and do what's next. For example, my first year of residency was one of my most stressful times. I might get called to see three people at once: Mr. A with shortness of breath, Mrs. B with chest pain, and Mr. C with leg pain. Rather than letting myself feel overwhelmed and stressed, I focused my attention on taking care of one person at a time. I might ask Dr. Y to see Mr. A, then I would see Mrs. B, and then Mr. C. Alternatively, I might quickly check one patient to see that he was stable, then go to examine the next patient, and then return to the first. The point is doing what is next and focusing on one thing at a time.

A Relaxation "Quickie"

In Western culture, we tend to think of the mind and body as separate. However, distress manifests with both mental agitation and muscular tension. As we calm our minds, our muscles will usually relax and, as we calm our muscles, our minds will often become more focused. Therefore, combining a technique to focus the mind with a technique for relaxing your muscles can be very effective in dealing with distress. If you do not have time for a long sitting or walking meditation, try this interesting and effective exercise to quickly reduce your level of stress:

This exercise is useful since it can done quickly and in any posture including sitting, standing or lying down. With each inhalation, notice your abdomen gently go out. With each exhalation, relax a different muscle group. For instance, with the first exhalation, you might relax your jaw; with the second, your neck; with the third, the little muscles between your eyes; with the fourth, your shoulders; and with the fifth exhalation, your back. You may try another muscle group, such as your arms or legs. It will not be long until you are feeling more relaxed.

Summary

1. Mindfulness consists of two very simple steps:
    A. ***Letting go of thoughts of how the present moment should be different.*** This includes thoughts of how your body should feel differently and/or how your particular circumstances should be different.
    B. ***Focusing on the present moment.*** It is particularly effective to focus on your breath and, even better, to breathe using your diaphragm. It is also effective to focus on any present input to your senses such as taste, touch, smell, vision, or hearing.
2. Notice if certain muscle groups tend to get tense during stressful times. If so, as soon as stress becomes apparent, do steps "A" and "B" described above and then focus your attention on those muscle

groups. Allow the muscles to relax just as you did with the meditation. Do not resist the sensations. Relaxing a particular muscle group is easiest if you do it as soon as you notice the stress.

3. Ideally the above steps should be done *quickly*. As soon as a thought of resistance appears, let it go. Do not let the cycle of stress (Figure 4) go on for long.

4. The above steps should be done *repetitively and regularly*. Mindfulness is a lifetime practice and a lifetime challenge. Each resistant thought you have gives you more opportunity to practice letting thoughts go. Even a small increase in the amount of time that you are mindful can dramatically improve the way you handle stress.

5. *Continue to set goals for the future.* In certain cases, changing our external environment is an extremely important way to deal with stress. However, realize that the present can only be the way it is. It is essential to learn to enjoy the process of change.

6. Learn to *use your energy,* instead of resisting it.

7. *Take appropriate precautions for your future, and use mindfulness to deal with worrying.*

8. *Mindfulness skills can be used to deal with habitual behaviors.*

9. *Focus on doing one thing at a time.*

10. *Assign certain events to be reminders to breathe mindfully.*

Richard was feeling progressively more anxious and overwhelmed at work. He said that, at times, he felt like a "deer frozen in a car's headlights — too anxious to move." After we talked, Richard made a realistic plan of what he could accomplish at work and prioritized the planned tasks. In addition, he planned to notice the thoughts that occurred when he felt stressed. He might notice the thought, "I'm overwhelmed." As soon as he noticed that thought, he would let it go and focus on his breathing, taking slow, diaphragmatic breaths. If the thought "I'm overwhelmed" came up again, he would again, patiently, let it go. As time went on, Richard also noticed thoughts like, "I don't like being here," "This is too hard," and "I hate this knot in my stomach." Each time he noticed one of these thoughts, he would let the thought go and focus on his breath. He would not resist the way his body felt. Instead of dwelling on everything he had to do, he would focus on doing the very next task. The more he did this, the more he found that he started enjoying his work and his stress decreased.

Probably several times a week, I have a patient with a problem very similar to Jim's problem. He was very uneasy at the beginning of our first visit. He eventually revealed that the main reason for the visit was a problem with sex. For the most part, his life was going well. He had recently married and had previously enjoyed an active sex life with his wife. Approximately one month before our meeting, however, he had been particularly stressed and was unable to obtain an erection. Ever since that time, he could either not obtain an erection during sex, or, if he did obtain one, he would lose it quickly. Nonetheless, Jim would frequently wake up with a normal, strong erection.

I explained to Jim that some men have trouble obtaining erections because the blood vessels or nerves going to the penis are damaged. An example of this might be a 75-year-old man with a long-standing history of poorly controlled diabetes. With other men, the predominate factor is psychological. In other cases, there are men in a gray area, in which a combination of these two factors are responsible.

Since Jim did have normal erections when he woke up at night, I suspected that his blood vessels and nerves were not damaged and that the primary problem was stress. Like most men, Jim had had an experience in which he had been unable to have an erection. Instead of shrugging it off as something that most men experience on occasion, Jim had become very worried about it. The next time he had sex, all he could think about was whether his erection would occur, so, of course, it did not. If he did get an erection, he would fixate on how it was doing. Normally, the intensity of an erection waxes and wanes during sex. But with Jim's anxiety about it, he would panic as soon as his erection was less intense, and then lose the erection altogether.

After our visit, Jim worked with the meditations on CD 1. He learned to gently let distracting thoughts go and put his attention on his wife instead of his erection. At our follow up visit, three weeks later, Jim's problem was much better, despite his unfilled prescription for Viagra.

To end this chapter, I'd like to share a quotation by Lao Tzu that is thousands of years old:

In Spring, hundreds of flowers,
In Autumn, a harvest moon,
In Summer, a refreshing breeze,
In Winter, snow will accompany you.
If useless things do not hang in your mind,
Any season is a good season for you.

Notice that Lao Tzu did not say "if useless things do not come to your mind." He said if "useless things do not **hang** in your mind, then any season is a good season for you." It is how we deal with the thoughts that we have that can bring us back to enjoying the present moment.

I have found that, at any given moment, if I choose to, I can be creative enough to find something to be stressed about. If I try hard enough, I can always worry about some future situation, be worried that I have acted inappropriately in the past, or wish that the present moment were different. At any given moment, I have the choice as to whether I will dwell on these thoughts or enjoy the present.

In a given moment, our thoughts of discontent may seem to be unique, but they are usually nothing really special. Likely they are very similar to thoughts we have had in our past and will have in our future. What is special is that, within each moment, is a test of how you want to spend that moment, and, as the moments add up ... how you want to spend your life.

Is this one issue worth having a life of distress? Wouldn't you rather have one of enjoyment? Set the precedent for how to handle the thoughts and issues in your life now. The only time you can choose to be mindful is right now. *Do not waste this moment; choose mindfulness right now!*

Exercises

In addition to reading about mindfulness, it is important to develop an experiential understanding of mindfulness. Tracks 2 through 4 of CD 1, and Track 1 of CD 2, include several exercises designed enhance your understanding of the techniques and ideas described in this chapter. It would be ideal to listen to those exercises now. The exercises can be done in one day or over a series of several days.

The first exercise allows you to you practice letting thoughts go. During the "letting go meditation," a variety of thoughts are introduced which could potentially cause you much stress. However, by learning to let go of the thoughts, people invariably feel much more relaxed by the end of that meditation. Again, it is not the thoughts that cause stress, but rather what you do with the thoughts that causes stress. Subsequently, walking and eating meditations are included. A short stretching meditation that can easily be done in a chair is next.

---

[10] Hanh, Thich Nhat. *Peace is Every Step.* New York: Bantam Books, 1991, pp. 26–27.

[11] *Ibid.* pp.18–20.

[12] *Ibid.* pp. 33–34.

5

⚙⚙⚙

Change Your Thoughts

*What disturbs people's minds is not events
but their judgements on events.*

EPICTETUS 100 A.D.

I n 1955, Albert Ellis, Ph.D. began popularizing the field of cognitive therapy, and came up with the ABC's of how our thoughts affect our emotions. When an event happens, he referred to it as the **antecedent,** or **A.** The event is often followed by an emotional **consequence,** or **C.** For instance, **A** might be your boss yelling at you. If you become upset, that would be the consequence, or **C. A** causes **C,** right?

According to the theories of cognitive therapy, the answer is not that simple. The reason you got so upset was not just from the antecedent (**A**), but mainly from a set of irrational beliefs we'll call **B.** To summarize, **A** (the antecedent) triggers **B** (the irrational beliefs), which in turn triggers **C** (the consequence). Perhaps when your boss yelled, you had a series of thoughts: "I can't do anything right .... I'll probably get fired .... I'll never get another job .... He probably thinks I'm a total failure ...." A yelling boss may be annoying, but it is the irrational beliefs that follow that cause you to feel miserable.

Ellis recommended adding a **D** to the ABC's, suggesting that we can and should **dispute** the irrational beliefs. In reference to the above example, such **D** thoughts might include: "I made one mistake; that does not mean I do everything wrong." "I've done most of my work correctly, and

I doubt that I'd get fired for doing one thing wrong." "If I did get fired, it might be a little difficult, but I'd find another job." "He just yelled at me today. Maybe he is having a bad day. I won't assume he thinks I'm a failure." Disputing the irrational beliefs will most likely decrease your stress, anger, frustration, and/or sadness.

Aaron Beck, M.D. and David Burns, M.D. further popularized cognitive therapy. In his book *Feeling Good,* Burns categorizes irrational beliefs, or what he calls "cognitive distortions."[13] By categorizing the irrational beliefs, we can more easily recognize them.

If your thoughts are clouded with cognitive distortions, it is like viewing the world through a cloudy, distorted lens. The cognitive distortions make situations seem worse than they really are. Burns discusses several cognitive distortions (italicized below) that are related to each other. It is not hard to see how a stream of thoughts may flow from one cognitive distortion to another:

- *All-or-none thinking:* If you do not perform perfectly, you think of yourself as a total failure.
- *Overgeneralization:* If one thing goes wrong, you start thinking, "Nothing goes right."
- *Magnification* or *catastrophizing:* One simple mishap is thought to be a catastrophe.
- *Minimization:* You do not pay attention to a variety of things that have gone right or you minimize their importance.
- *Labeling or mislabeling:* One or two relationships do not work out and you find yourself thinking that you are unlovable. You do not perform perfectly at one job and you mislabel yourself as worthless. If other people's behavior disturbs you, you mislabel them as jerks, rather than trying to understand their points of view.
- *Personalization:* You blame yourself for an event that was not your fault. For instance, it is not uncommon for a child to blame himself for his parents' divorce.
- *Emotional reasoning:* You assume that, because you feel bad, you are bad. An example would be thinking: "I feel sad and worthless. Therefore, I must be worthless."

- *Jumping to conclusions:*
  - *Mind-reading:* You assume that you know what another person is thinking, when you truly do not. The person who did not say "hello" might not dislike you. He or she may have been preoccupied, may not have seen you, or may have been too shy to speak up.
  - *Fortune telling error:* You upset yourself by predicting the worst possible outcome for the future.
- *Should statements:* You dwell in the past, thinking about how you should have acted differently. It is very easy to have 20/20 vision in hindsight, but that is not available to us as we make our choices. Dwelling on *should statements* is counterproductive. "Should I have acted in one way or another?" is a pointless question. It only serves to keep you from enjoying the present moment. Let go of any "should conversations" as soon as you notice them. The only "should questions" that might be useful to ask is: "How should I act now or in the future?" Rather than dwelling in the past, you can accept your past decisions and learn from your mistakes.

To help yourself dispute irrational beliefs, it is helpful to categorize the cognitive distortions. Initially charting the thoughts out on paper may be helpful. Just writing down an irrational belief often allows you to see how truly irrational it is.

Let's apply this technique to the earlier example:

Situation	Emotion(s)	Automatic Thoughts	Type of Cognitive Distortion	Dispute (Rational Response)
Your boss yells at you.	Sadness, anger frustration	"I can't do anything right."	All-or-none thinking	"I did one thing wrong, but I've done a lot right."
		"He probably thinks that I'm a total failure."	Mind-reading	"He was annoyed at this one event. I cannot assume that he thinks that I'm a total failure."

As you gain experience in learning to quickly recognize cognitive distortions, charting them will usually not be necessary. In time, you will automatically recognize cognitive distortions, and quickly act to let them go or dispute them.

Mary's experience illustrates several cognitive distortions. When I first saw her, Mary had recurring episodes of stress and depression that would last for months. The episodes seemed more understandable once we reviewed some of the thoughts that typically accompanied these periods. As soon as she would start feeling depressed, Mary would think, "Oh, no! Here it goes again – another two months of stress and depression." At these times, Mary would often focus on a recent past relationship in which she was abused. She would think, "I never should have stayed in that relationship. I really can't be in a good relationship. I feel really down. I really am worthless."

Once we had talked about the impact of cognitive distortions, Mary made the following chart. Making the chart allowed Mary to see the patterns that had worsened her stress and depression. Seeing these distortions made it easier for her to shift her thinking.

Emotions	Thoughts	Type of Cognitive Distortion	Dispute
Stress Anxiety Depression	"Another two months of stress."	Fortune telling	That happened in the past, but not necessarily now. Let's reframe the situation and make it a challenge to have this episode be much shorter.
	"I never should have stayed in that relationship."	Should statement	Reframe: instead of berating myself, I will focus on the lessons that I learned in the relationship. For instance, I will not tolerate abuse in future relationships.
	"I really can't be in a good relationship."	All-or-none thinking	I made mistakes with the past relationship, but I learned from it.
	"I feel really down. I'm worthless.	Emotional reasoning	Just because I feel bad does not mean that I am bad or worthless.

Two of the most frequent cognitive distortions are overgeneralization and all-or-none thinking. When you find yourself making general statements about a problem or failure, it is essential that you dispute the generalization.

Catastrophizing is a cognitive distortion that is particularly prevalent when people feel stressed. Saying strongly negative phrases to yourself or to others can dramatically increase your stress. Putting situations into a more rational perspective can help alleviate the stress. (This is described further in Chapter 8).

Just replacing the strongly negative phrases with less forceful or dramatic phrases can help with stress as well. Typical catastrophizing may include thoughts such as: "This is horrible;" "It's a catastrophe;" "I'm ruined;" or "I can't believe it happened." Your stress would decrease if you replaced those phrases with the somewhat milder phrase, "It was unfortunate."

If you tend to catastrophize, the phrase "It was unfortunate" may be a very useful addition to your mental vocabulary. Sometimes asking if a problem will really matter in ten years will also help with catastrophizing.

Denise worked setting up displays at a store. One day, she had spent all day setting up a display exactly as she was instructed and, at the end of the day, her boss changed her mind about what she wanted. Denise was very upset. She found herself thinking, "This is horrible. I can't believe this could happen." When she realized that she was catastrophizing, she corrected herself in a way that was much closer to the truth: "It's inconvenient that I will have to set up a new display." Once she realized that the situation was not the "end of the world," she felt much better.

Another way to deal with catastrophizing is to practice reframing.

Reframing

The harder you fall, the higher you bounce.
ANONYMOUS

The process of reframing involves placing a new frame or context around a particular situation. Initially, you might view a difficult task as an *objectionable chore*. By reframing, the task it can be viewed as a *challenge*.

Two men who had numerous occasions to reframe their highly public lives, ultimately came to these conclusions:

We are continually faced by great opportunities
brilliantly disguised as insoluble problems.
LEE IOCOCCA

The pessimist sees difficulty in every opportunity.
The optimist sees opportunity in every difficulty.
WINSTON CHURCHILL

Thomas Edison worked long hard, hours and had many failed attempts when trying to invent the incandescent light bulb. These failed attempts would have discouraged many people. However, Edison said, "I am not discouraged, because every wrong attempt discarded is another step forward."

How many times have we berated ourselves for not doing something correctly, or sometimes even for not doing something perfectly? Instead of interpreting an effort as a failure, it is much more productive to reframe an unsuccessful effort as an opportunity to ask, "What can I learn from this?" What would otherwise be a time of despair can become an opportunity to learn.

> Failure is only the opportunity to begin more intelligently.
> *HENRY FORD*

> Success is the ability to go from one failure to another
> with no loss of enthusiasm.
> *WINSTON CHURCHILL*

> Forget about the consequences of failure. Failure is only a temporary change in
> direction to set you straight for your next success.
> *DENIS WAITLEY*

> An expert is a man who has made all the mistakes
> which can be made in a very narrow field.
> *NIELS BOHR*

Some research suggests that people with a lot of hostility are more likely to get heart disease.[14] By reframing an encounter with a rude person, we can actively dissipate our hostility. I ask members of my stress management classes, "Who here has ever been rude?" Typically, everyone in the class raises his/her hand. Next I ask, "When you have been rude, is it usually when you are happy and feeling your best?" The unanimous answer is "no." This unofficial study yields very convincing results. If 40 out of the 40 people in class-after-class are suffering, in one form or another, when they are rude, then perhaps we can extrapolate further: *When most people are acting rude, they are usually suffering, in one way or another.* Bear this in mind when an acquaintance is rude. Instead of immediately reacting with anger, realize that he or she might not be doing well. Did the bank teller's wife just file for divorce? Did your boss just find out about her sister's breast cancer?

Realize that much of our communication involves people that we really do not know that well. Even with the people we know relatively well, we only are aware of a small amount that is going in their lives and their minds. We only know the "tip of the iceberg." If someone is rude, almost undoubtedly, they are suffering in one way or another. At times, it may be helpful to ask if something is bothering them. Other times, it might not be a good idea. However, even in those cases, it decreases your own stress and hostility to appreciate that the behavior that on the surface represents rudeness on a deeper level represents suffering.

What about the people who seem to be rude most of the time? Well, perhaps they are unhappy most of the time. For instance, many people suffer from clinical depression. Another reason some people appear rude is a difference in communication styles. A stereotypically fast-talking New Yorker may seem rude to someone not accustomed to that communication style.

One woman in my class was a supervisor for a group of receptionists. The receptionists voiced their frustration about customer complaints. The supervisor advised that they *look at each complaint as an opportunity to make a positive difference in someone's life.* Another woman supervised a staff who answered the phones at a psychiatric hospital. Her employees were bothered by the rude calls they were receiving. Therefore, she decided to start a contest. The person who received the rudest call of the week would win a prize. Instead of getting annoyed and taking the nastiness personally, they were almost happy to get the rude calls. It did not take much of a prize to help them gain some new perspective.

Some people get annoyed when they have to do some extra walking. They could reframe the situation and be thankful for the opportunity to get some exercise. There is nothing more ironic than people fighting to park as close as possible to the entrance of their health club, so they can exercise on a treadmill.

For the next example of reframing, imagine that you are in a grocery store checkout line. You pick the shortest line because you are in a rush. However, the line turns out to be the slowest. You find yourself wondering how you always seem to pick the slowest line. You get annoyed as you watch the customer in front of you, who starts paying with a credit card, but then changes his mind and decides that paying with a check would be better. Then he remembers the 12 coupons in his pocket. So the cashier starts over and the customer writes a new check. Your blood pressure continues to rise. How would you reframe this situation?

In these busy times, many of us rush from one task to another. We seldom have time without demands. Reframe this time at the grocery store as just such a time. View it as an opportunity to focus on your breathing, reflect on your plans, list those aspects of your life for which you are grateful, or indulge the opportunity to just look over a magazine.

We find ourselves waiting for a variety of activities through the week. It's easy to create a lot of stress during these waits. Whether you're put on hold while calling an office, at the Department of Motor Vehicles, at the bank, or in a traffic jam, it is key to be able to reframe these waits as opportunities to take a time out from the daily rush of activities. Once you do this, potential times of stress become opportunities to relax.

How else might we reframe the wait at the grocery store? Some Buddhists believe that all of our suffering is caused by our mind. They believe that if we train our minds effectively with meditation, we will no longer have suffering. When a problem arises, rather than getting upset, they view it as an opportunity to train their minds. Even if you do not share the belief that you can be totally free from distress by training your mind, you can, hopefully, start appreciating the power your mind has over stress. By doing so, you can *reframe what would have been a difficult situation as an opportunity to train your mind.*

As you notice the tension building in the grocery store checkout line, you can reframe the situation and be thankful for the time to train your mind. This same technique of reframing can be used when the situation is more serious, such as being laid off from a job. Every hardship can be seen as an opportunity to train your mind. Each challenge you meet makes you more prepared for the next one.

Let's think about our emotional and physical pain in another way. A weightlifter's muscles really hurt during a workout and often after a workout. If, out-of-the-blue, someone's biceps started aching like a weightlifter's muscles, they would knock on a doctor's door without delay. However, the weightlifter does not complain to the doctor. In fact, he or she may even enjoy the pain. Why is that? To the weightlifter, the pain has a meaning. It means that the muscles are growing and getting stronger. If the pain had no meaning, it would be something to be avoided.

We have all gone through painful experiences, and when we can find meaning in those experiences, it helps to decrease our suffering. Perhaps you are stressed or distressed about your physical conditioning — not liking the way you look or feel. You can dwell in this distress or use that feeling to motivate you to start an exercise program. Once you make that decision, it helps alleviate your suffering. Perhaps you suffer from a painful condition, such as rheumamtoid arthritis. Even in this situation, you can choose to dwell in the stress and pain, or decide that your condition challenges you to find the best medical and behavioral treatments. Not only that, the pain might have further meaning if you started a support group to help others, or if you decided to help with the local Arthritis Foundation. By reframing the pain to find some sort of meaning, your suffering will decrease.

I would prefer it if neither myself nor my family ever had any serious medical problems. However, my luck in that regard has not been perfect. Sooner or later, we all will see pain and illness in our families. It slightly decreases my pain to find meaning in the fact that any pain I have experienced increases my empathy for other people. It makes me a better physician, communicator and human being, when I learn how to deal with my own pain. In this regard, I have learned more as a patient or family member of a patient than I have in most of my medical school classes.

Earlier I talked about distress (bad stress) and eustress (good stress). I suggested tht one way to turn distress into eustress was to "use the stress." For this discussion about pain, it may be useful to coin the terms "dispain" and "eupain." If we can find some meaning or use for the pain we may be able to transform this dispain into eupain. The dispain consists of dwelling in suffering. The eupain is the pain in which we find a meaning — the pain that motivates us and helps us grow.

So many times we set goals or we have dreams, we have plans and we work our tail off and it doesn't come out the way we want. And a lot of people come out of the situations disillusioned or angry or resentful or frightened or frustrated. They look for someone to blame. Sometimes I really, truly believe that not getting your goal is part of the design. It's part of the game plan. Causing you to dig inside and discover more of yourself; to really begin to use your real capacity as a human being; those traits that are within you and only expand when you are challenged — when demands are made upon them. I believe that God is not as interested in our convenience than in our character. And I also believe that if something did not happen right away when you wanted it..., it does not mean that it is not going to happen.
It's really a test of how committed are you?
ANTHONY ROBBINS [15]

That which does not overcome me makes me stronger.
NIETZCHE

Sally was diagnosed with an enlargement in her cheek that was thought to be a tumor. She was scheduled for an MRI scan and was terrified of the prospect of lying still in a tube for forty minutes to be scanned. As Sally put it, she was working herself into a "frenzy" about the test. She was about to ask her doctor for some Valium, when she decided to reframe the situation instead. She reminded herself that she was always busy, doing one thing or another. She never had time just to sit and reflect about the things and people in her life for which she was grateful. The MRI scan could be a special time of solitude where no one would interrupt her. These thoughts gave a new meaning to the scan and soothed her anxiety, so that she was able to tolerate the procedure well. The tumor turned out to be benign. Since then, whenever Sally is in a traffic jam or similar circumstance, she reminds herself to appreciate her solitude and the opportunity to reflect on her life.

When our twins were eight months old, my wife and I planned a trip to visit relatives. This trip required our family to drive over 300 miles. After approximately one hour of driving, we had a blowout. That's right – while we were on a busy freeway, our right rear tire shredded. It was very understandable when my wife said, "This is a nightmare; it is horrible." It was a bad situation, but catastrophizing would not make it better. So I said, "This is definitely not ideal, but we will manage." I was able to slowly drive on the shoulder and get to a small road that was much less busy.

As my wife watched the boys, I emptied the back of the station wagon (which had been carefully packed to the brim) to get to the spare and then proceeded to change the tire. Together, my wife and I reframed the situation and agreed that it had been lucky that the flat had happened while we were together (as opposed to her being alone with the boys); that it had happened during the daytime; that it had not been raining; and that there had been a small street, a mile up the road, that had made it much safer for us to stop than it would have been to change the tire in the middle of a freeway. (Previously, my wife had been very astute in pointing out the danger to all of us of getting rear-ended by someone going 70 mph if we stayed on the shoulder for a significant length of time.)

An important exercise on CD 2 Track 2 will help you practice reframing and explore ways to combine reframing and mindfulness.

Internal vs. External Locus of Control

The best years of your life are the ones in which you decide your problems are your own. You do not blame them on your mother, the ecology or the president. You realize that you control your own destiny.
ALBERT ELLIS, PH.D.

Though we travel the world over to find the beautiful, we must carry it with us or we find it not.
RALPH WALDO EMERSON

Things turn out best for the people who make the best of the way things turn out.
JOHN WOODEN

A happy person is not a person with a certain set of circumstances, but rather a person with a certain set of attitudes.
HUGH DOWNS

Another important concept in cognitive therapy is "locus of control." Having an "external locus of control" implies thinking that your happiness and satisfaction primarily depend on the external environment. In contrast, having an "internal locus of control" implies thinking that most of your happiness and satisfaction depend on the choices that you make and the way you view life.

Jon Kabat Zinn titled a book *Wherever You Go, There You Are.*[16] His reasoning for the title was that, wherever one goes, he or she takes with them certain attributes. Those attributes will help determine whether they are "stressed out" or enjoy life.

On a PBS special, Wayne Dwyer once told a story of a visitor to a town asking one of the long-term residents, "What is this town like?" "Well," the resident asked, "What was your old town like?" The visitor said, "People were angry, no one was nice, and it just was not a very fun place at all." The resident said, "Well, our town is a lot like that."

A week later another visitor asked the same resident, "What is this town like?" The resident asked again, "What was your old town like?" The second visitor said, "In my old town, people were great. Everyone really looked out for their neighbors and cared about each other. It was a really pleasant place to live." The resident responded, "Our town is a lot like that." The way we view our circumstances has at least as much to do with our happiness as does the circumstances themselves.

W. Mitchell speaks throughout the world about how he has handled his challenges. In the early 1970's, he had a severe burn accident affecting 65% of his body, including his face and hands. Just as his life was starting to go well again, he had a second accident, leaving him paraplegic. At first, he found his wheelchair a prison, keeping him from doing the things he wanted. Later, he reframed this, and the wheelchair became a wonderful apparatus that helped him travel throughout the world. Before the accident he "could do 9,000 things; after the accident 8,000 things." He chose to celebrate the 8,000 things he could do, not dwell on the 1,000 things that he could not do. His philosophy is embodied in the title of his book: *It's Not What Happens to You. It's What You Do About It.* *

It might not be surprising to learn that people with an internal locus of control tend to handle stress better. In fact, one of the purposes of this book is to give people a more internal locus of control when it comes to dealing with stress. Hopefully, next time your stress level is high, you won't just say, "Poor me," or "I can't do anything about it because it's his or her fault." Instead, you might try some of the stress management techniques that are discussed in this book.

---

*I do Mitchell's wonderful story a disservice with this brief summary. For an inspirational read, get *It's Not What Happens to You. It's What You Do About It*, by W. Mitchell. Arvada, CO: Phoenix Press, 2001. Or check out his audio tape or video tape at www.wmitchell.com.

There are certain things that we may say or think that undermine our internal locus of control. For instance, if I say, "He *made me* angry," I give all the responsibility for my anger to whomever "he" is. Additionally, if I say, "I got angry *because* she left the top off the toothpaste," I have no other choice but to be angry. That sentence implies the one appropriate response is to be angry.

Instead, if I say or think, "She left the top off the toothpaste *and* I got angry," I admit to other options. I could have thought it was funny and laughed. I could have been sad, or not cared. The point is that, by restating the thought in a different way, I give myself a choice in how I respond. This might sound insignificant, but next time you think or say someone *made you* feel a certain way, or you feel that way *because* someone did something, try correcting yourself. You may be surprised at the subsequent change in your attitude.

There are other ways in which we limit ourselves with our language. Examine the statements: "I can't do math," and "Every time my boss criticizes me, I get very upset." Compare them with, "In the past I have had trouble with math," and "In the past when my boss criticized me, I would get very upset." As you can see, the latter statements leave open options for how to act in the future.

Thoughts can unconsciously confine you to a certain view of reality. However, when you take a step back, you will recognize that the walls that formed that reality were just thoughts. Then you can see that, instead of being overwhelmed, you had a thought that you were overwhelmed. Instead of the traffic making you angry, you had a thought that the traffic made you angry.

Taking this step back allows you to let certain thoughts go in order to enjoy the present moment. You may also dispute or reframe thoughts to improve your management of stress.

---

[13] Burns, David D. *Feeling Good.* New York: Avon Books, 1980, pp. 42–43.

[14] Braunwald, Eugene, M.D. (editor); *Heart Disease: A Textbook of Cardiovascular Medicine,* 16th ed. New York: W. B. Saunders Company, 2001; pp. 2244–2245.

[15] Robbins, Anthony. *Get the Edge,* San Diego: Robbins Research International, Inc., CD 7, Track 2 (available at www.gettheedge.com)

[16] Jon Kabat-Zinn, *Wherever You Go There You Are; Mindfulness Meditation in Everyday Life.* New York: Hyperion, 1994.

6

Slow Down

Half our life is spent trying to find something to do
with the time we have rushed through life trying to save.
WILL ROGERS

For fast-acting relief, try slowing down.
LILY TOMLIN

What is the use of running when we are not on the right road?
GERMAN PROVERB

Most men pursue pleasure with such breathless
haste that they hurry past it.
SOREN KIERKEGAARD

Slow Down, Baby you're going too fast
You got your hands in the air
With your feet on the gas
You're 'bout to wreck your future
Running from your past.
INDIA.AIRE
(SONG "SLOW DOWN" ON THE ALBUM VOYAGE TO INDIA)

ccording to a popular story, two cardiologists, Drs. Friedman and Rosenman, pondered the rapid rate at which their waiting room chairs were wearing out. Looking into their waiting room, they noticed a very impatient, anxious group of patients sitting almost on the front edges of their chairs. This observation gave them the idea that there is a certain personality style associated with a higher risk of heart disease. They labeled this personality style the "Type A personality." Following this observation, the two cardiologists along with a biochemist, Dr. Sanford O. Byers, began exploring the relationship of personality style and heart disease. Several studies did indeed show a relationship to Type A personality and heart disease.[17]

People with "Type A personalities" continuously struggle to accomplish more and more. Unlike people with Type A personalities, people with Type B personalities tend to be more mellow and laid back. With the Type A personality there is a sense of time urgency, often when there is no real reason to rush. The time urgency includes: talking very quickly and increasing the rate of another's speech (e.g., finishing other's sentences), driving and eating fast, and doing multiple tasks at once.

Type A people tend to be more aggressive and hostile. Although there has been some recent controversy as to the effect of Type A behavior on heart disease, the effect of excessive anger and hostility has been clearly shown to be related to heart disease in several studies. One study followed 1305 men for 7 years. The men with the greatest levels of anger had 2.66 times the risk of developing a heart problem.[18]

The Type A personality can be changed. The aggravation, impatience, anger, and irritation associated with this personality style do not usually produce good results at work nor at home. The researchers advise people with Type A personalities to take time with friends, avoid interrupting people, practice waiting in line and driving in the slow lane, and practice eating slowly and fully tasting food.

There are many other ways to integrate relaxation into your life. The therapeutic benefit of owning a pet is becoming increasingly recognized. In fact, "pet therapy" is becoming popular in hospitals and nursing homes around the country. We are likely to get even more benefit from the love we give a pet than from the love we receive from the pet.

Other advice includes learning to empathize with others, taking time for "cultural activities" (such as museums, art, and music), and avoiding trying to do many tasks at once. (Perhaps it is reasonable at work to dictate or write a "to-do list" while you are just sitting on hold for 10 minutes. This is still, in a sense, doing one thing at a time. However, when I found myself dialing a phone, dictating as I waited for someone to answer, and then forgetting whom I had called — well, that was too much.)

If it means rushing through the work day at a very harried pace, interrupting people and trying to do several projects at once, just to get home thirty minutes earlier, it probably is not worth the additional stress. Although it is important to have time at home, it is better to enjoy working an 8½ hour day, than to spend an 8 hour day in distress. People with a Type A personality often worry about wasting time, so I found this quotation from a lecture by researcher Diane Ulmer, R.N., M.S. to be particularly relevant: *"A day wasted by not enjoying it is the real waste of time."* In fact, I might add that a *moment* wasted by not enjoying it is the real waste of time.

> Enjoy the little things, for one day
> You may look back and realize they
> Were the big things.
> *ROBERT BRAULT*

Ulmer feels that the major factor in the development of the Type A personality style is low self-esteem and a continuing need to prove oneself. A low self-esteem cannot be improved by the frantic pursuit of material objects or achievements. It is important to have an inherent sense of self-worth. Most people in my classes say that they are willing to believe that all of us have inherent worth, independent of any accomplishments. If you have a thought otherwise, remember it is just a thought that can be let go, and then you can return to enjoy the next breath. When it surfaces again, you gently let it go again.

> No one can make you feel inferior without your consent.
> *ELEANOR ROOSEVELT*

Cindy worked in a retail store. Like many people in the retail business, she is often rushed for time. One day, a demanding customer was taking a long time at the store. Instead of spending an extra two minutes addressing this person's concerns, Cindy became impatient. By cutting her time with this customer short, she saved those two minutes. However, later that day she remembered what she'd done and it bothered her. She spent some time justifying her actions to herself, then spent some more time feeling bad, and wondering if she had been rude.

The next day, the customer complained to Cindy's supervisor. Cindy then had to spend an extra 30 minutes writing a response to his complaint. Cindy might not have done anything technically wrong, but in the long run she only saved two minutes by rushing a conversation with the customer and those two minutes ultimately cost her much more time feeling stressed about the interaction and responding to the complaint.

Sometimes rushing not only increases our stress, but really does not save any time at all. The book *The House of God* is a sarcastic novel that looks at the difficult life of medical residents.[19] It claims that experienced residents often teach new residents certain "laws" of residency. One of the laws has to do with how one should act at a cardiac arrest (when a patient's heart stops): "At a cardiac arrest, the first procedure is to take your own pulse." For someone that has never "run a code" (i.e., directed the staff in caring for someone having a cardiac arrest), this law probably seems like a joke in poor taste. Only those of us that have run a code understand it.

When someone's heart has stopped there is the temptation to frantically just try to do something. However, when you are frantic in a code, you are inefficient and will be more likely to make a mistake. Even when someone's heart stops, it can be much more effective for a doctor to take 2 or 3 seconds and one diaphragmatic breath, before acting. That way the doctor can remember his training and act efficiently and thoughtfully. I would not actually take my pulse. A one-minute delay is a bad idea. But a couple of seconds to take that diaphragmatic breath could help save a life.

Consider this: there are not many emergencies more pressing than someone's heart stopping; yet, even then, it makes sense to take one diaphragmatic breath before acting. If you need to push someone off the train tracks before a train hits them, you might not have those two seconds. For almost all of our other "personal emergencies" we can and should spare at least that amount of time.

In our frantic lives, we sometimes have to remind ourselves that we're not in the middle of an emergency. Several years ago, I occasionally worked weekend shifts as a doctor in an understaffed urgent care center. Since there were no scheduled appointments, patient waiting times were often long. One Sunday, there were an unusually large number of patients to be seen, and the wait was well over two hours. I found myself exhibiting "Type A" behavior — frequently interrupting patients and rushing them along. Suddenly I realized that no one was dying.

I decided that, on Monday, I would advise the administration that we needed more staff on weekends in the future. But, in the meantime, I needed a strategy for the current weekend. My Type A strategy of rushing and interrupting patients was only saving a few minutes, at best. And it was unfair to the patients. If someone had already waited two hours, the last thing he or she needed was a doctor who interrupted every other sentence.

Instead, I decided to shift my perspective and give each patient a more considered interaction with me. Seeing a doctor who listened empathetically would certainly be worth an additional 10-minute wait to these patients. On that long day, I saw over 40 patients. However, I was not stressed, and the patients did seem more appreciative, despite their wait, since their problems were carefully and considerately addressed.

---

[17] Dr. Friedman admits to an upholsterer pointing out the excessive wear, but claims that their revelation about the Type A personality did not occur until a little later.

Friedman, Meyer, M.D. and Diane Ulmer, R.N., MS. *Type A Behavior and Your Heart.* New York: Ballantine Books, 1984.

[18] Kawachi I, Sparrow D, Spiro A, et al: "A prospective study of anger and coronary heart disease: The Normative Aging Study." *Circulation* 94:2090–2095, 1996.

[19] Samuel Shem, *The House of God.* Dell Books, 1981.

1

Keep Life in Perspective

Rule #1: Don't sweat the small stuff.
Rule #2: It's all small stuff.

DR. MICHAEL MANTELL

One of the more important ways to cope with stress is to learn to keep your problems in perspective. One day a student became very upset, so he went to speak with his teacher. The teacher asked him the question, "If you had a billion dollars and you lost five dollars, would you be upset?" The student said, "Of course not." The teacher then said to the student, "You are a billionaire." The student then understood that when he considered all he had to be thankful for — his family, friends, and health — he was, in a sense, a billionaire. The next time something went wrong he thought to himself, "Five bucks," and smiled. In most instances, if we can take a step back and put a problem in perspective, our stress level decreases markedly.

Gratitude

There are only two ways to live your life — one is as if everything is a miracle, the other is as though nothing is a miracle.

ALBERT EINSTEIN

We can only be said to be alive in those moments
when our hearts are conscious of our treasures.

THORNTON WILDER

One of the most effective ways to keep problems in perspective is to remember to appreciate what we have. Often, we ignore many of the important things in life for which we could be grateful. This is partly because our brains cannot focus on too much information at once. If we are in a room illuminated by fluorescent lights, after a while we no longer hear the hum of the lights. If we are at a dinner party with four simultaneous conversations and we focus on one conversation, we do not hear the others. Our brains can only process a relatively small amount of the information gathered by our senses at any one time. If we consider all the memories, plans, and other information that our brains contain, it becomes obvious that we can focus on only a minute fraction of our brain's content at any one particular time. We can use this quality of our brains to our advantage by choosing what we want to focus on.

Often, it is helpful to remind ourselves of what we have to be grateful for throughout the day. You can contemplate this whenever you are feeling down or regularly at the end of your meditation.

Imagine the most awe-inspiring scenic view that you have ever seen. Recently, I was at a restaurant that had such a view. On three sides of the restaurant were breathtaking vistas of the Pacific Ocean. When the waiter was asked what it was like to work in the environment, he said that, most of the time, he forgot about the view. Only occasionally would he remind himself to appreciate the scenery.

There are many positve aspects of our lives to which we have grown accustomed. Like that waiter, we need to remind ourselves to appreciate our blessings. List the things in your life for which you are grateful: your health, the people in your life, and even a warm shower. Be grateful that you have food to eat. If you can see, be grateful for your vision; if you cannot see, be grateful for your hearing. If you have trouble hearing, be grateful for your senses of touch and taste.

Throughout the day, repeating thoughts such as "I feel privileged for (blank)" or "to have (blank)" can help put the stressful events of your life in perspective. In addition, those statements have the added benefit of helping you focus your mind to enjoy the present moment. For instance, when we make a statement of gratitude or give a prayer of thanks before eating a bite of food, we are more likely to eat that food mindfully.

If only people who worry about their liabilities would think about the riches they do possess, they would stop worrying. Would you sell both your eyes for a million dollars... or your two legs... or your hands ... or your hearing? Add up what you do have, and you'll find that you won't sell them for all the gold in the world. The best things in life are yours, if you can appreciate yourself.
DALE CARNEGIE

When we respond to the challenges life hands us, we can find positive aspects of unfortunate situations. Helen Keller wrote, "I thank God for my handicaps, for through them, I have found myself, my work, and my God." Our culture tends to be preoccupied with looks. Golda Meir said, "Not being beautiful was the true blessing... Not being beautiful forced me to develop my inner resources. The pretty girl has a handicap to overcome."

In her book *Simple Abundance*,[20] Sarah Ban Brethnach strongly recommends making a "gratitude journal." At the end of the day, she recommends writing down five things for which you are grateful. Some days it may be something small, like the new birdhouse you bought; other days, you might list more serious items, such as health and family. You might review yesterday's five items in the morning. Before you know it, you will have a whole book full of items for which you can be grateful. You can refer to that book whenever you want.

I think starting a gratitude journal is an excellent idea. Take a moment to list some of the people and parts of your life for which you are grateful. As a bare minimum, fill in the spaces below now. During difficult times, it's important to refer back to this list or to add to it.

1. _____

2. _____

3. _____

4. _____

5. _____

6. _____

7. _____

8. _____

9. _____

10. _____

11. _____

12. _____

13. _____

14. _____

15. _____

16. _____

17. _____

18. _____

19. _____

M. Greg Stathakis has been teaching high school for 37 years. He is a dedicated teacher and has a passion for his work. He not only wants to teach English, but also wants to leave his students with something more. For example, when a student says something negative, Greg asks the student to say five positive statements about his or her life ... then five more positive statements. He hopes his students will develop a reflex to be grateful.

To experience how a sense of gratitude can positively affect your life, try the following experiment. Several times an hour, over the course of a day, look for something for which to be grateful and actually say one of the following statements to yourself:

- "I am grateful to have (blank)"
- "I feel privileged to have (blank) in my life"
- "I am so lucky to have (blank)."
- or pray, "Thank you for (blank)."

Say the statements with feeling. As you say how grateful you are for a friend or family member in your life, visualize his or her face. Think of different special moments. Think of your health, your ability to see, hear and/or feel beauty. Be thankful for the food on your plate and the ability to taste good food.

During the day that you purposefully repeat those statements to yourself, notice how you feel. If you make this a regular practice it will make a very positive difference in your life.

Purpose and Altruism

Dennis was a 65-year-old gentleman who had been retired for ten years when he came to see me. Most of Dennis' stress revolved around his chronic back pain. The pain had first started after an injury about 20 years before. Since that time, he had tried multiple pain medications, attempted physical therapy several times, and had gone through two back surgeries. He had also participated in an intensive, six-month pain management program with no success. His pain was managed only by huge daily doses of morphine.

On one visit, Dennis shared with me that his need for the pain medication had decreased dramatically. He was now only taking one morphine pill every two weeks. Instead, he was taking a considerably weaker pain pill, once every two to three days. He felt incredibly well and, most days, did not need any pain medicine at all. To what did Dennis attribute this remarkable change? Dennis had started a job in which he sold equipment to disabled people. Not only did he really enjoy the job, he truly felt that he was making a positive difference in many people's lives. He felt wonderful and had at least a 90% improvement in both his pain and his stress.

After Victor Frankel survived the horrors of a Nazi concentration camp during World War II, he realized that all of the survivors had one trait in common — a strong sense of purpose.

All of us can gain perspective in our lives by developing a sense of purpose and a sense of making a positive impact in others' lives. Choose a job and hobbies for which you can have a passion and can hopefully make a difference in others' lives. Anne Frank said, "How wonderful it is that nobody need wait a single moment before starting to improve the world."

Whatever work you do, do it with integrity and in a way that contributes to others. Helping others shows you what is important and quiets your mind from its preoccupation with complaints about relatively small problems. William Bennet said, "There are no menial jobs, only menial attitudes." You can be bored as you sell flowers at a flower stand or you can seek to make each person you deal with a little happier. You can indirectly bring beauty to others as the flowers are given as presents and shared with others. You can struggle working in construction or you can take pride in acquiring skills and building to the best of your ability.

If you seek happiness for yourself,
you can have everything in the world and still be unhappy.
But, if you seek happiness for others, you'll find
happiness yourself. That's the way it is.
TRULSHIG RINCHOPE

Is the above quotation true or does it just sound nice? There are many unhappy rich people. The most fulfilled people have learned the joy of true compassion. Caring for others gives us the opportunity to stop the chatter about what we "lack." It provides us a stronger sense of purpose and helps us put our lives in perspective. It lets us experience the joy of contributing and compassion.

I don't know what your destiny will be,
but one thing I know: the only ones among you who will be truly happy
are those who will have sought and found how to serve.
ALBERT SCHWEIZER

This is the true joy in life, the being used for a purpose
recognized by yourself as a mighty one; the being thoroughly worn out
before you are thrown on the scrap heap; the being a force of nature
instead of a feverish selfish little clod of ailments and grievances
complaining that the world will not devote itself to making you happy.
GEORGE BERNARD SHAW

From what we get, we can make a living:
what we give, however, makes a life.
ARTHUR ASHE

If you can't feed a hundred people, then just feed one.
MOTHER TERESA

The research confirms that altruism is associated with health. For instance, epidemiologist James House studied 2,700 men in Tecumsah, Michigan. Men who did not volunteer were two-and-a-half times as likely to die during the study period than men who volunteered at least once a week.[21]

Altruism can take many forms. You can help others in small everyday ways or take on much more ambitious projects. Richard Bach, in his book, *Illusions,* wrote: "Here is a test to find whether your mission on Earth is finished: if you're alive, it isn't."*[22]

It is worthwhile to take a moment to reflect on what activities you can feel naturally passionate about. Incorporating those things into your work or other parts of your life can help bring perspective and joy.

Humor

Laughter is a form of internal jogging. It moves your organs around. It enhances respiration. It is an igniter of great expectations.
NORMAN COUSINS

Another way to gain perspective is through our sense of humor. A cartoon I particularly like shows a contemplative Ziggy who says, "You better learn to laugh at your problems; the rest of the world already is." Our

---

*It is also important to care for ourselves, for if we do not, we will not be in the best shape to help others. This is discussed further in Chapter 8.

sense of humor can help carry us through those times which might otherwise be much more difficult. Develop your sense of humor by watching funny movies, reading the comics and humorous books, or searching for new jokes on the Internet. You might even want to practice telling jokes, so you can make others laugh.

Humor can often be found in stressful situations. "To defuse potentially stressful situations with humor, Joel Goodman, director of The Humor Project, in Saratoga Springs, New York, recommends imagining how your favorite comedian would react to the same situation."[23] When one thing after another goes wrong, it's easy to become frustrated. Sometimes frustration can be turned around by throwing a little humor in.

> "Once I was traveling to give a lecture. The plane was late, and everyone else's luggage came off before ours. Somewhere across town, there were several hundred people in a rented hall waiting for me to give a talk — perhaps on the importance of being on time — and it was getting later and later. Finally our luggage started to arrive ... One suitcase had sprung open, and clothes were spread all over the conveyer belt. Another piece of luggage was obviously damaged. The people traveling with me were more and more upset. Finally I said, 'Relax, this is funny. In a few weeks we'll be telling stories about tonight and laughing about it. If it'll be funny then it's funny now.' And we started looking at the situation as if it were a Woody Allen movie. When some of the luggage didn't arrive, we smiled. When the car rental company didn't have our reservation (or cars), we laughed. When we heard there was a taxi strike, we howled."[24]
> *JOHN ROGER*

People were very stressed at Sally's work place. It seems that much of the staff was on vacation in August. The remaining staff was, therefore, getting behind in processing orders. As they got further behind, they had to respond to more and more phone calls about the late orders. This further delayed the process. Several hour-long and seemingly irrelevant work meetings made the situation worse. Sally designed a sign for the bulletin board that said, "Seven-hour meeting today to discuss why the work is backlogged." The humor seemed to draw the staff together and lighten the mood, though Sally is currently unemployed ... (just joking!)

It is essential to learn to laugh at yourself. Learn to laugh at your occasional neurotic behavior and perceived shortcomings.

> He who laughs last didn't get it.
> HELEN GRANGREGORIO

> Laugh and the world laughs with you. Snore and you sleep alone.
> ANTHONY BURGESS

Things Change

When the outlook seems gloomy, we may also gain perspective and comfort from the Buddhist doctrine of "impermanence." There is one constant principle in the universe and that principle is "things change." Time does not stand still. Life constantly changes. When people are depressed, it sometimes feels as if the situation will never change and the depression will last forever. However, you may rest assured during the hardest times that, as the saying goes, "This too shall pass."

It is comforting to remember that when life seems difficult, it often eventually works out, one way or another. Another much-repeated saying tells us, "When one door closes, another opens." Or as Helen Keller said, "When one door closes, another opens; but often we look so long at the closed door that we do not see the one which has opened for us." We have all been upset over a particular event, and then later realized that it was actually good fortune in disguise. Not infrequently, I have heard of someone being laid-off from a job only to eventually find a job that was much better.

My father-in-law was moving from northern to southern California. He rented a truck and a trailer. Just as he was ready to leave, he found that the trailer was incompatible with the truck. As a result, the brake lights wouldn't work. He was forced to leave the trailer in northern California, knowing that he would need to drive an extra twelve hours roundtrip to retrieve it. As he set out without the trailer, the truck had a tire blowout. He pulled to the side of the road easily. He later learned that, if he had had a blowout while driving with the trailer, his truck would have likely jackknifed and he could have been in a very serious accident. The seeming misfortune of an incompatible trailer might have saved his life.

Sometimes a children's story has an important message for adults. In *It Could Have Been Worse,* a young mouse becomes upset on several occasions as he trips or falls down.[25] He has one "mishap" after another, so he thinks he is having a terrible day. However, he never seems to notice that each time he falls, it helps him narrowly miss being caught by one of several predators. Each time he is slightly bruised, but still alive. This story shows children (and their parents) that what seems like an unfortunate event on the surface may, in reality, be a truly fortunate one. Sometimes we, like the mouse, do not know the whole story.

Many religions teach that when circumstances do not look good on the surface, we must trust there is a larger plan. Having this view helps people cope with disappointment and also decreases worry by increasing confidence that they can handle whatever the future brings. Some people may put this trust in God and others may trust their own ability to deal with whatever "comes down the pike." Either way, this type of trust can be tremendously comforting in times of potential stress.

I asked God for strength, that I might achieve;
I was made weak, that I might learn humbly to obey.
I asked for health, that I might do greater things;
I was given infirmity, that I might do better things.
I asked for riches, that I might be happy;
I was given poverty, that I might be wise.
I asked for power, that I might have the praise of men;
I was given weakness, that I might feel the need of God.
I asked for all things, that I might enjoy life;
I was given life, that I might enjoy all things.
I received nothing that I asked for, but everything I had hoped for.
Almost despite myself, my unspoken prayers were answered.
I am, among all people, most richly blessed.
ANONYMOUS

You don't always get what you want.
But if you try sometimes, you might just find,
you get what you need.
THE ROLLING STONES

Some of God's greatest gifts are unanswered prayers.
GARTH BROOKS

What the caterpillar calls the end of the world,
the master calls a butterfly.
RICHARD BACH

Sally told me that, as a young mother, she was overwhelmed with stress. Her young son had been diagnosed with diabetes. This required extra care and contributed to extra worry in her already busy life. She was having trouble functioning day-to-day. Finally, she said she "gave the problem to God." What I think she meant by that was that she decided to trust that God would help to take care of the situation in one way or another. The solution would all be part of God's plan. When Sally started to feel too stressed, she would tell herself that she was "giving her problem to God" and she would have a tremendous sense of relief.

The ultimate way to gain perspective may be to remind ourselves that our time on Earth is limited. Do not waste time complaining about the "small stuff." Instead, enjoy the ride, including all of the bumps and curves in the road.

It's only when we truly know and understand that we have a limited time on earth — and that we have no way of knowing when our time is up — that we will begin to live each day to the fullest, as if it was the only one we had.

ELISABETH KUBLER-ROSS

Sarah was frustrated with her work. Her boss had made several unreasonable demands. She was required to work long hours and her work was unappreciated. Sarah's boss would yell at the staff for no good reason. Sarah was becoming more and more stressed at her job. To put things in perspective, I asked Sarah to think about what was the worst that would happen if she stood up to her boss. What would happen if she did not agree to the unreasonable demands and if she asked instead that she be treated with the respect that she deserved? After thinking for a while, Sarah decided that the worst that would happen would be that she would be fired from a job she hated, and be able to collect unemployment while she sought a better job. It was unlikely that she would actually be fired, but in this case, "the worst" that could happen would not be so bad. After considering this, her stress at work decreased.

---

[20] Breathnach, Sarah Ban, *Simple Abundance*, New York: Warner Books, Inc., 1995.

[21] Hafen, Brent Q., Keith J. Karrren, Kathryn J. Frandsen, and N. Lee Smith, *Mind/Body Health*. Boston: Allyn and Bacon, 1996, p.403.

[22] Bach, Richard, *Illusions: the Adventures of a Reluctant Messiah*, New York: Dell Publishing Co., Inc., 1997, p.159.

[23] 30 Ideas to Reduce Stress at www.thriveonline.com/health/stress.30tips.html

[24] McWilliams, John-Roger; Peter McWilliams, *You Can't Afford the Luxury of a Negative Thought*. Los Angeles: Prelude Press, Inc., p. 277.

[25] Benjamin, A.H.; Tim Warnes, *It Could Have Been Worse*. Waukesha, WI: Little Tiger Press. 1999.

8

Improve Your Lifestyle

At the end of you life, you will never regret not having passed one more test,
not winning one more verdict, or not closing one more deal.
You will regret time not spent with a husband, a friend, a child, or a parent.

BARBARA BUSH

Balance

One of the keys and challenges to a healthy lifestyle is to balance all of the different areas of your life. When we take time to develop multiple aspects of our life, including relationships, family, work and hobbies, any single problem can seem less stressful. In other words, we do not have "all of our eggs in one basket." If our bosses yell at us, we can still get satisfaction from our friends, family, and/or hobbies.

There is no better time to find balance in your life than the present. Not infrequently, I see patients with two children working stressful, 70-hour weeks. As we contemplate the last 10 or 20 years of our lives, we might be surprised at how quickly the time went. As we get older the time seems to go faster and faster. I have not heard anyone on his or her death bed say that they wished that they would have spent more time working. If you don't take the time to enjoy life now, when are you going to do it?

Maintaining balance in our lives sometimes requires us to resist our cultural preoccupation with money and possessions. We are continually bombarded by advertisements telling us what we need to purchase to be happy. Most material objects at best bring very brief happiness. We would be much happier if we learned that we do not need most of what the advertisers say we need. Once your basic needs are met, obsession with material objects does not bring happiness. Most of us know rich people that are unhappy. If we do not know them personally, we hear of wealthy celebrities who suffer with depression and even commit suicide. On the other hand, there are many people of much more modest means who thoroughly enjoy life. Too often, we find ourselves in extra financial stress, since we have been sold on the idea that we need that extra fancy car or need expensive clothes. Then we need to work many more hours, possibly multiple jobs, to meet expenses.

Stress can often be reduced by simplifying your life. For instance, you might find that you are better off with a smaller house that is easier to maintain and has a smaller mortgage. This arrangement might allow you to work less and spend more time with family, friends, and hobbies. Another way to simplify your life is by giving away or selling old objects that are never used (after consulting with your spouse and family, of course; let's not start any huge fights).

Who is rich? He that rejoices in his portion.
BENJAMIN FRANKLIN

He is richest who is content with the least.
SOCRATES

I believe that a simple and unassuming manner
is best for everyone, best both for the body and the mind.
ALBERT EINSTEIN

The trouble with the rat race is that, even if you win, you're still a rat.
LILY TOMLIN

Bonnie's parents were well-off and she had become accustomed to a relatively costly lifestyle growing up. She and her husband worked hard to continue that lifestyle and, before she knew it, she was working four jobs. Although none of the jobs were full-time, the combination was much more than full-time. After taking my stress management class, she started to realize that her lifestyle was costing her more than just money. Her stress was markedly reduced when she made some changes, including selling her expensive car and quitting two of her jobs.

One way to improve the balance of your life is to set aside time away from work in order to have time focused on family, friends and/or spirituality. Many religions recommend a Sabbath day. When we are younger, we sometimes do not see the wisdom of traditions. As we gain more experience, it may make a lot more sense to make sure that at least one day is set aside for activities other than work. At least one day set aside from work and at least some time each day away from work will help keep your life more fulfilled and balanced.

Balance is important not only between our work and family life, but also between different parts of our family life. A good friend told me that she and her husband had had some marital tension. She wondered about the possibility of counseling. Her husband suggested that, instead of spending money on a counselor, they spend money on a babysitter for a date night once a week. Counselors help many people learn to communicate better. However, this couple was communicating fairly well. They just needed some time devoted to their marriage, as opposed to having all of their energies just spent on work and children.

Balance is important between all of the aspects of our lives, including work, marriage, children, relaxation, hobby and exercise. Stop competing with others trying to show how much stress you can tolerate. Instead, create a life in which you take pride in your balanced, healthy lifestyle.

Time Management

Simplifying our lives also involves time management. Many of us attempt to fit more into our schedules than is necessary. If we have an 11 a.m. appointment, we might find ourselves trying to do six errands before the appointment. It is best to adjust your schedule so you're not stressed by constantly rushing or running late. Plan to do just the two or three most important errands before the appointment and make a more realistic schedule for the other errands.

One way to deal with a stressful schedule is to create some "margin." Richard Swenson, M.D. describes margin as "the space between our load and our limits."[26]

We would try not to leave ourselves only 10 minutes to make a connection between two airline flights. If we did, at best, we would have to race to make the second flight. At worst, we would miss the flight. If we try to continually run our lives at maximum capacity, without leaving any room for unexpected occurrences, or even room to relax once in a while, we will burn out. In other words, avoid scheduling yourself at 100% capacity. Give yourself that "margin."

Dr. Swenson points out that, today, people are much busier than at any previous time in history. Our progress was supposed to give us all sorts of free time, but instead, we are working more and have less margin than our ancestors. Therefore, when compared to the rest of history, this current cultural norm is not so normal at all. We, as a culture, are out of sorts with what is healthy.

Why should we be in such desperate haste to succeed, and in such desperate enterprises? If a man does not keep pace with his companions, perhaps it is because he hears a different drummer.
HENRY DAVID THOREAU

In *Don't Sweat the Small Stuff with Your Family,* Richard Carlson, Ph.D. described the maintenance of the Golden Gate Bridge. He stated that "the bridge is painted almost every day of the year."[27] In other words, as soon as they finish painting the bridge, they need to start all over again.

Dr. Carlon compares this to the maintenance of a house. There is always something that could be done. In fact, there are many areas of our life similar to painting the Golden Gate Bridge. You can decrease your stress by realizing that no matter how hard you try, your "in-box" will never be empty. You can always find some task to do. Instead of stressing about it, enjoy the process.

This never-ending list of tasks makes setting priorities that much more important. Not infrequently, we procrastinate and delay the activities that are most important. The real stress is the dread of having some important task loom over us. Often, once we get started, we actually enjoy the task. One solution starts by taking the time to list your life goals and priorities (such as education, family, health, exercise, etc.). The next step is to make a "to-do list" and then, to make a daily schedule that includes the most important priorities. You can then rank the items "A" (most important), then "B," and finally "C" (least important). Make sure you include the A priorities in your day, every day. Do not think that marking things with an A ranking means they have to be hard work. Exercise, adequate sleep, and a relaxation exercise are examples of moderate, but advisable, "A priorities."

It is important to include activities in your day that you enjoy doing. Psychologist Robert Ornstein, Ph.D. and physician David Sobel, M.D. talk about "healthy pleasures" as a way of keeping stress in check.[28] This may include a variety of activities from relaxing in a bathtub to taking a hike. Ideally, think of at least some activities that you enjoy that do not require a lot of time. Then include these activities throughout the day. More examples of healthy pleasures could be listening to music, spending time with your pet, watching a sunset, getting a massage, giving a massage, making love, slowly enjoying a meal, reading a good book, viewing or creating art, gardening, etc. Activities which include nature may be particularly helpful. Take time now to list activities that you enjoy.

1. _____

2. _____

3. _____

4. _____

5. _____

6. _____

7. _____

8. _____

9. _____

10. _____

11. _____

12. _____

13. _____

14. _____

15. _____

16. _____

17. _____

18. _____

19 _____

20. _____

The use of a scheduling system will help prevent the stress of forgotten or delayed errands. Local office supply stores or bookstores usually sell items that vary from simple calenders to more elaborate scheduling systems. A relatively simple system is to have a calendar and a daily "to-do list" that you can update each day. A useful plan might be to draw a line through activities as they are accomplished and circling ones that are to be postponed until later. Other people use a PDA or palm-sized computer in order to manage their schedule.

Another method to increase your effectiveness with time management is to learn to delegate responsibilities. Once people do delegate a task they are sometimes too quick to reassume the responsibility. You may hear them say, "If I don't do it myself, it won't be done right." Delegation can make your life a lot easier, if you train people properly. It can be a tremendous asset to your life, if you allow people the time to learn the task and give them feedback when necessary.

Many people spend several hours a day watching television. Go ahead and watch a television show on occasion, but avoid spending hours "surfing" through the channels. Spending hours watching shows you don't enjoy — just to get up and realize all the chores left to be done — does not relieve stress. Also, watching a lot of television violence does not contribute to long-term well-being. Be aware of what you feed, not just your children's minds, but also your own.

A study in the *Journal of the American Medical Association* examined the association of sedentary activity with obesity and diabetes in over 50,000 women.[29] You might not be surprised to learn that each two-hour-a-day increment of sitting at work was associated with a 5% increase in obesity and 7% increase in diabetes. Interestingly, each two-hour increment of sitting in front of a television was associated with a 23% increase in obesity and 14% increase in diabetes. Why was the television worse? It is unclear. It could be the commercials, encouraging you to eat, or a variety of other factors. The point is, too much television is not good for you.

Many families have a television in every room and habitually turn on the set as they walk into the room. Giving away a television or two may be an effective time management and stress management strategy. Do an experiment: strictly limit your television for one week and you may never return to watching the same amount.

Michael was a college student who came to an appointment complaining of back and abdominal pain. He had already been to several specialists and had multiple tests. He feared that the pains might be caused by some sort of cancer. I reviewed with him that the previous tests had eliminated the possibility of cancer. His pain was real, but the causes of it were irritable bowel syndrome and back spasm, both made worse by stress.

We first explored Michael's thought processes. He would start thinking about how he was "overwhelmed" by his class assignments. When he noticed the thoughts that he was overwhelmed, I suggested he let those thoughts go. Instead of worrying about the entire semester of work, he now could focus on doing the next task. When he did this, he started actually enjoying the tasks that he had formerly dreaded. He also unplugged the television. If there was an occasional important show to watch, he plugged the television back in. However, with the set unplugged, there was less temptation to take an impulsive two-hour television break from studying. Instead, after every hour or two of studying, Michael would spend 5 or 10 minutes stretching, listening to music, or playing with his dog. He also started to schedule regular times to swim and meditate. On Michael's next visit, his back pain was gone and he reported that his abdominal pain was "95 percent better."

Exercise

As I discussed in Chapter 2, stress has been described as the "fight or flight response." Regular exercise is a good way to use some of the excess energy generated by stressful situations. Some people use exercise on an as-needed basis; that is, the effects of a hard day at the office may be alleviated by a good jog after work. However, it is ideal to exercise on most days.

Regular exercise is made easier when people find types of exercise they enjoy. Exercise does not have to be limited to running or jogging. It can be walking, swimming, biking, hiking, playing racquetball, basketball, etc. You do not have to elevate your pulse excessively. Raising your pulse rate to 60–80% of your maximal predicted pulse for 20 to 30 minutes most days is sufficient. (In order to calculate your maximal predicted pulse, subtract your age from 220. For instance, if you are 40 years old, your maximal predicted pulse would be 220 minus 40 which equals 180. Your target heart rate would 60–80% of 180 which equals 108–144. Your pulse can usually be felt at the thumb side of your wrist or at the groove on the side of your neck (only check one side at a time). To calculate your heart rate, count the number of pulsations you feel in 15 seconds and multiply by four.

Put another way, you don't have to run as hard as you can. Taking a brisk walk is excellent exercise. People over 35, or with medical problems, such as heart disease, should discuss an exercise program with their healthcare provider before beginning.

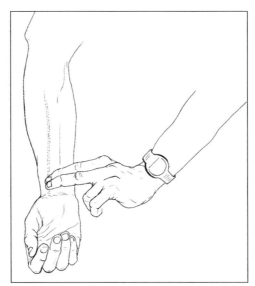

Figure 5: You can take your pulse by lightly placing the index and long fingers of one hand on the thumb side of the opposite wrist. Count the number of beats in 15 seconds and multiply by four to obtain the pulse rate.

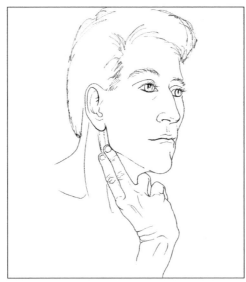

Figure 6: You may also take your pulse by lightly placing your index and middle fingers on the groove on the side of your neck. (Only check one side at a time.)

Does it seem impossible to fit exercise into your schedule? Don't give up easily. The ideal time might be first thing in the morning, at lunch time, or after work. Try taking a regular walk with the dog or a baby stroller. If the weather is bad and you don't want to go outside, a home exercise machine might be helpful. Consider walking to the store or, if possible, biking to work instead of driving. When my twin boys were infants, either one or the other would often get cranky in the early evenings. Taking one of them out for a walk in a sling (baby holder) would calm the baby and give me a chance to get exercise. You might plan a similar exercise routine each day or you might prefer variety. Either way, if you make exercise part of your daily routine, you are more likely to do it rather than just think about it.

Ted usually tried to go for a jog after work. However, he noticed that one thing or another always seemed to get in the way. One day it might be additional paperwork from the job; another day, it might be a family obligation. Ted was in the habit of setting the alarm for 6:10 am and hitting the snooze button once or twice before getting out of bed. He would then go downstairs and make some coffee. He would slowly wake up and get ready to be at work at 8:00 am. One evening he decided to try something different. He set his alarm just ten minutes earlier and visualized getting out of bed as soon as the alarm went off. The next morning he did just that. He put on his running clothes and was out the door in minutes, jogging in the crisp, fresh air. Ted felt so refreshed from his morning run that he found he did not need his usual coffee. In fact, the next week, he spent his morning "coffee break" relaxing with some fragrant herbal tea, instead of nursing his third cup of coffee. Once he began to experience the invigoration of exercise, he looked for new ways to add it into his life – not as a chore, but as a pleasurable activity. During the weekends, he soon began to take a longer hike or bicycle ride. He found that, as soon as he recognized exercise as something that added genuine quality to his life, it was possible to fit it into his schedule.

If you are not currently exercising regularly, take a moment now to write a list of exercises that you might enjoy:

1. _____   6. _____

2. _____   7. _____

3. _____   8. _____

4. _____   9. _____

5. _____   10. _____

When will they fit into your schedule?

Sunday: _____

Monday: _____

Tuesday: _____

Wednesday: _____

Thursday: _____

Friday: _____

Saturday: _____

Avoiding Excess Alcohol, Caffeine, or Drugs

I saw a patient who was about 30 years old and was suffering from what appeared to be severe panic attacks. Before prescribing the medications typically used for panic attacks, I asked him how much caffeine he drank. "Three a day" was his answer. Three cups of coffee per day can certainly increase a person's anxiety level. Then, he clarified his response; it was three *pots* of coffee a day. People have varying sensitivities to caffeine. Even a cup or two a day can cause problems for some people. Caffeine is also contained in many teas, chocolate, and some sodas. Although caffeine can precipitate headaches for some people, a sudden reduction in caffeine intake may also result in headaches or fatigue for a few days. Therefore, some people choose to gradually reduce their caffeine consumption, instead of suddenly discontinuing it.

A glass or two of wine helps some people relax, but when alcohol is taken in excess, distress may worsen. Many heavy drinkers are surrounded by friends who also drink heavily, and may have difficulty recognizing that they have a problem with alcohol. Recovery from alcohol addiction often requires that people find new social support groups. Alcoholics Anonymous is one group that serves this function well.

Several so-called recreational drugs can also cause increased anxiety. Cocaine and amphetamines can cause severe anxiety and panic. Even a single use of these drugs can cause a heart attack or seizure. Illegal drugs are not the only drugs that make people anxious. Certain decongestants, asthma medications, antidepressants, and appetite suppressants can cause excessive anxiety in susceptible individuals. If you suspect this type of problem with a prescribed medication, discuss the issue with your doctor before discontinuing it.

Nutrition

I went on a diet. Had to go on two diets at the same time
'cause one wasn't giving me enough food.
BARRY MARTER

Good dietary habits are important for effectively dealing with stressful situations. Small, frequent meals are more beneficial than skipping meals. A nutritious breakfast can do much to decrease the stress in a day. By skipping breakfast, people tend to get low blood sugar. The low blood sugar may, in turn, increase certain stress hormones. It is not a surprise to most of us that hungry people tend to be stressed and irritable. Some people think that they might lose weight by skipping breakfast. Research by Mark Pereira, Ph.D. (sponsored by the American Heart Association) showed that people who regularly ate breakfast had a much lower incidence of obesity than people who did not regularly eat breakfast. People who ate breakfast regularly also had a lower risk of "insulin resistance." Insulin resistance, a condition related to diabetes, is a risk factor for stroke and heart attack. Eating a healthy breakfast low in saturated fats and sugars further lowered the risk of obesity and insulin resistance.[30] If there is absolutely no time for a meal, a meal substitute (such as meal drink or bar) would be better than skipping breakfast completely.

It is also important to avoid frequently eating foods loaded with sugar and to make sure that you include plenty of fruits and vegetables in your diet. Mindfulness is an important tool for healthy and enjoyable meals. Wine connoisseurs, for example, don't simply drink wine; they savor it — appreciating the color, bouquet, and every subtlety of the flavor. Bringing the same degree of mindfulness to other food and drink makes mealtime much more enjoyable.

Overweight people can especially benefit from eating mindfully. Before eating, take some diaphragmatic breaths and notice if you have any sensation of hunger. If not, postpone eating, if possible. Often we eat out of habit or to deal with stress, sadness, or other emotions.

Another modern day problem is the limited time we sometimes give ourselves to eat. As our lunch hours get crammed with paperwork and errands, we tend to inhale our food.

Make certain you schedule adequate time to eat and enjoy your meals. When you do eat, take the time to enjoy the food's aroma, texture, and taste. Too often we eat, but barely taste the food. We might watch television, think of the work day, or compare the food to an earlier meal.

When trying to lose weight, it is important to be mindful of the decreasing sensation of hunger. I advise people to stop eating every few bites, take some deep diaphragmatic breaths, and evaluate their level of hunger. Some people end their meal when they are "full," but by that they mean "stuffed." Rather, as the hunger sensation begins to subside, I advise people to stop eating. Put the food away and/or get up from the table to discourage continued nibbling. The sensation of being full grows for up to 20 minutes following a meal. This style of eating encourages the healthy routine of eating small, frequent meals. A guided eating mediation is included on Track 4 of CD 1.

Daily Relaxation Exercise

Short-term stress is usually not harmful. Health problems arise when anxiety and stress are prolonged. A daily relaxation exercise can help decrease the level of anxiety. Regular meditation can help lower stress levels significantly. There are several other types of relaxation exercises such as guided imagery, progressive relaxation, self-hypnosis, Tai Chi, and yoga. Many books and videos on these subjects are available.*

---

*For example, *The Relaxation and Stress Reduction Workbook* by Martha Davis, Ph.D., Elizateth Robbins Eshelman, M.S.W., and Matthew McKay, Ph.D. (See my suggested reading list for further details.)

Social Support

A friend divides your sorrows and multiplies your joy.
ANONYMOUS

There is nothing on this earth more to be prized than true friendship.
SAINT THOMAS AQUINAS

No medicine is more valuable, none more efficacious, none better suited to the cure of all our temporal ills than a friend to whom we may turn for consolation in time of trouble, and with whom we may share our happiness in time of joy.
SAINT AILRED OF RIEVAULX

Our quality of life and ability to handle stress can be enhanced by a good social support system. The benefits of a good support system range from an increased resistance to colds[31] to a longer life.[32] In a frequently quoted study, David Spiegel, et. al., studied the benefits of support groups for women with metastatic breast cancer.[33] One group in the study received standard cancer therapy; the other group received standard cancer therapy and also participated in support groups comprised of other women with metastatic breast cancer. The women in the support groups maintained a better emotional status and lived twice as long as the women who did not belong to support groups.* Several studies have correlated an improvement in social support with a decrease in the incidence of heart disease.[34]

It is more important to develop a few close friendships with people in whom you can confide, rather than having a long list of acquaintances. Our friends and our families are extremely important and should not be taken for granted. Be mindful to nurture your current relationships. In addition, establishing new relationships can also be important. Participation in adult education classes, churches, synagogues, or a variety of other activities may help you meet people with common interests. If you

---

*The dramatic change in life expectancy seen in this study has not yet been reproduced in other studies on breast cancer and social support, raising the possibility that there were many factors involved.

enjoy hiking, join a hiking group to meet people with a similar interest. Varying your routine can give you the opportunity to meet new people. One patient of mine went to the same church every Sunday for many years. When he finally went to another church for a change of pace, he met the woman who became his wife.

When my wife was 20 weeks (4½ months) pregnant with our twins, she developed premature contractions. She starting having up to 12 contractions in an hour. We knew that, if delivery happened any time before 24 weeks, we would lose both of our twins. Before 28 weeks, their outlook for being healthy would be risky. Even at 32 weeks, a stay in the neonatal intensive care unit would be very likely. So her premature contractions were extremely stressful for us, to say the least.

We employed several strategies to help with this stress. Among the most important was relying on social support. We got support from her physicians. We did our research and strictly followed her doctors' recommendations. My wife was amazing. She followed the orders for bed rest very strictly and took medication to decrease the contractions, as prescribed. We asked for support from family and friends. We resisted the urge to be "polite" and not accept help. Friends cooked meals. Family visited and helped my wife with bed rest. We found a support group for pregnant women on bed rest and learned what we could from them. (The group is Sidelines and information can be found at www.sidelines.org). We prayed. My wife learned and did self-hypnosis, and spent quiet time listening to relaxing music. When she relaxed in this way, she noticed the contractions seemed to decrease.

We are extremely thankful that my wife gave birth to two wonderful boys. If you have had one new baby, you know how much work is involved. Of course, taking care of twins is even more work. If ever the lack of sleep and amount of work became difficult, the greatest tool that helped us manage the stress was our gratitude for having our two wonderful boys

Our social support continued to be important after our boys were born. Our family and friends continued to offer help and we continued to accept it. We joined the local Mothers of Multiples group to help us with hints and support regarding raising twins.

People have a variety of emotions during a period of grieving and these emotions frequently change. They may include shock, sadness, anger, denial, and/or guilt. Social support is important in coping with stress, and also in dealing with these other emotions. Even after time does some healing, an event or memory can suddenly change a good mood to tears. Sometimes, the oddest thing can stir a memory out of the blue and the tears flow. As long as you do not resist the tears, the sadness usually passes.

When my father passed away, talking with family and friends was extremely helpful. My family and I took some time off work, so we could just grieve together.

Support from clergy was also helpful. During the funeral service, the clergyman said something that comforted me. My father could live on — not only in memories — if we made his great qualities our own. We talked of his kindness, honesty, and love of his family. If we make it a point to embody these qualities, our father would live on in us.

During another religious service, I heard a question that, for some reason, comforted me. Someone asked: If you could make the choice that no person currently living would ever die, but there could be no other baby born to enjoy life's pleasures, would you take that deal? I do not think that I would take that deal. And somehow, that notion helps me be a little more accepting of the cycle of life and death.

---

[26] Swenson, Richard, M.D. *Margin.* Colorado Springs, CO: Navpress, 2002.
Swenson, Richard, M.D. *The Overload Syndrome.* Colorado Springs, CO: Navpress, 2002, p. 13.

[27] Carlson, Richard. *Don't Sweat the Small Stuff with Your Family,* New York: Hyperion, 1998, p. 25.

[28] Ornstein, Robert and David Sobel. *Healthy Pleasures.* Reading, MA: Addison-Wesley, 1989.

[29] Hu, Frank B. Tricia Y. Li, Graham A. Colditz, Walter C. Willett, and JoAnn E. Manson "Television Watching and Other Sedentary Behaviors in Relation to Risk of Obesity and Type 2 Diabetes Mellitus in Women" *Journal of the American Medical Assoc.* 2003. Vol 289: 1785–1791.

[30] McNamara, Damien. "Regular Breakfast Eaters at Lower Risk for Obesity," *Family Practice News.* May 15, 2003, p. 10

[31] Cohen, Sheldon; et. al. "Social Ties and Susceptibility to the Common Cold." *JAMA,* 277:24 (6/25/97) pp. 1940–1945

[32] House, J. S.; Landis, K. R.; and Umberson, D. "Social Relationships and Health." *Science,* 241 (1988): 545.

[33] Spiegel, D.; Bloom, J, R.; Kraimer, H. C.; and Gottheil, E. "Effect of Psychosocial Treatment on Survival of Patients with Metastatic Breast Cancer." *Lancet,* (1989): 888–891. The results of this study have not been reproduced, raising the possibility that there are many factors involved.

[34] Braunwald, Eugene MD (editor); *Heart Disease: A Textbook of Cardiovascular Medicine* 16th ed.; New York: W. B. Saunders Company, 2001; pp. 2247–2248.

9

⚮

Improve Your Communication

If you want to be listened to,
you should put in time listening.

MARGE PIERCY

If there is any great success in life, it lies in
the ability to put yourself in the other person's
place and to see things from his point of view —
as well as your own.

HENRY FORD

Much of our stress centers around our relationships with others. Therefore, improving our ability to communicate should improve our ability to manage our stress. Carl Rogers, Ph.D., the father of "humanistic" or "client-centered" psychology, taught that there are three basic components of good communication: unconditional positive regard or acceptance, empathy, and genuineness. Unconditional positive regard or acceptance is illustrated by the following Rogers' quote:

"One of the most satisfying feelings I know — and also one of the most growth-promoting experiences for the other person — comes from my appreciating this individual in the same way that I appreciate a sunset. People are just as wonderful as sunsets if I can let them be. In fact, perhaps the reason we can truly appreciate a sunset is that we cannot control it. When I look at a sunset, as I did the other evening, I don't find myself saying, 'Soften the orange a little on the right hand corner, and put a little purple along the base, and use a little more pink in the cloud color.' I don't do that. I don't try to control a sunset. I watch it with awe as it unfolds. I like myself best when I can appreciate my staff member, my son, my daughter, my grandchildren, in this same way."[35]

Unconditional positive regard has two elements. One element is to be "mindful" as you listen to someone; that is, to be present and pay close attention to the other person during the conversation. The other element involves the acceptance of a person as he or she is. People have different styles. Some are like a sunset — mellow and easy to be with. Others are like the Rocky Mountains — rough and gruff. The Rocky Mountains can be a beautiful and awe-inspiring place to visit. However, if you are in the mountains and spend all of your time wishing that you were watching a sunset at the beach, you will not be happy.

Accepting people as they are, and learning to enjoy their individuality, does not mean you accept everything they do. As a saying goes, you can "love the sinner without loving the sin." Accepting someone also does not require you to spend time with that person. If you are at a zoo, you may see a lion and really admire it, but don't jump into its cage. On occasion, one might hear of a woman whose husband repeatedly beats her, but continues to stay with him because she says she loves him. This is a case where it would be better to love from afar.*

Another key component to good communication is empathy. Empathy sometimes gets confused with pity, which is very different. With pity, you might look down on another person. With empathy, you put yourself in the other person's shoes. Empathy underlines our commonality. Even if we have not gone through a death in the family, we have all had losses and know what loss feels like. We may never know exactly what another goes through, but we can try to get close. In fact, one of the few good things about our painful times is that they allow us to identify more closely with another's pain. Sometimes the best training a doctor receives is when he/she or his/her family member is a patient. Where there is an empathetic listener, both people in a conversation benefit.

---

*For brevity, I have oversimplified the predicament that certain abused spouses find themselves in. For further support, contact the National DomesticViolence Hot Line at: 1-800-799-SAFE. For hearing impaired TDD at: 1-800-787-3224. For emergencies: dial 911.

Empathy is not only an effective communication tool, but is also an effective stress management tool in its own right. When we can try to see life from another's point of view, we may notice our own anger, hostility, and stress fading. Empathy allows us to be more patient with friends, family members, and strangers that we interact with throughout the day, as well as people that we've never talked to. I once had a discussion with a patient with severe emphysema who claimed he was so upset by slow drivers that he went back to smoking. If this same patient had been able to empathize with the predicament of the other drivers, he may not have felt as compelled to jeopardize his own health.

In 1995, a man sped through an intersection in Baltimore after the light had turned red. He hit the driver's side of my mother's car and almost killed her. She fractured three ribs on each side, fractured her pelvis, and punctured both lungs. The injured lungs could not function correctly and predisposed her to subsequent life-threatening pneumonia. She spent two months in an intensive care unit on a breathing machine — unable to talk — and an additional several months recovering. Miraculously, with the help of a dedicated medical team and a lot of prayer, she recovered and is now well. But, as you might suspect, when she first resumed driving, she was nervous and sometimes drove slowly.

The next time that you get annoyed at the driver in front of you, realize he or she may have a good reason for his or her behavior. Empathy allows us to recognize that there are many other stories besides our own.*

Genuineness, the third essential component of good communication, follows naturally when unconditional positive regard and empathy are present. It is not genuine to tell someone how wonderful he or she is, while simultaneously thinking that he or she is a "jerk." However, it is genuine to have a thought that someone is a "jerk," let that thought go, and then relate to them in an empathetic and accepting manner.

---

*There is a very legitimate worry about drunk drivers and the high percentage of deadly accidents they cause. I have wondered if there are also a lot of accidents and deaths caused by someone trying to make the yellow light. Certainly there are a lot of accidents caused by sleep-deprived drivers. So, if you have been drinking, don't drive; if you are tired, pull over and rest; and if you see a yellow light, stop if possible. It's too easy to temporarily lose respect for the amount of damage, loss of life, and family pain that can be caused by the cars we drive.

With empathy, acceptance, attentiveness, and genuineness, our ordinary conversations can be transformed into something warm, intimate, and beneficial to both parties. Even when the situation is sad, we can have healing conversations that bring us closer to one another.

In addition to the healing potential, there are other practical benefits of empathy. Let's pretend that your job is to make the schedules for two bosses: Boss A and Boss B. One day, Boss A says to you that you should schedule their appointments every 30 minutes. The next day, Boss B tells you that their appointments should be scheduled every hour; therefore, you schedule people every hour. Four days later, Boss A storms into your office and yells: "What an idiot! Can't you do anything right? I gave simple instructions to schedule people every 30 minutes and you couldn't even follow them."

There are several ways that you might respond to this situation:

1. You say to yourself: "Poor me. I always get these unreasonable, awful bosses. I'll probably lose the job." (Let's call this the **victim response** — not very productive.)

2. You say to your boss: "You think I'm the idiot! You are the stupidest person I've ever met." (the **aggressive response** — don't be surprised if you get fired and have trouble getting a good reference letter.)

3. You say to the boss: "Yes, Boss A. No problem. I'll do it however you want. Sorry to inconvenience you." At the same time you say to yourself: "Well, he wants people scheduled more frequently. Let's see how he likes it to have them scheduled every 10 minutes." (**Passive-aggressive** — may be fun in the short term, but in the long term it is unlikely to be to be productive.)

4. You say to your boss: "I understand why you would be upset. If I asked an employee to do something, and it looked like he disregarded my request for no reason, I would be angry as well. However, shortly after you gave your instructions, Boss B told me to schedule people every hour. There was no right answer. I was in a "no-win" situation. If you and Boss B can decide together on my instructions, I'll be happy to comply."

(Notice how you **first empathized with your boss,** so he could feel acknowledged, and **then later asked him to empathize with you.**)

Barbara was having a lot of trouble communicating with her nine-year-old daughter. Barbara felt the trouble was that they both had short tempers and would yell at each other. When I asked more about it, I found that Barbara complained that her daughter Robin would say things like, "All the other mothers spend more time with their daughters." Barbara would argue that it was not true, since she knew that most of Robin's friends' mothers had full-time jobs. Barbara needed to work full-time to make ends meet. I suggested that next time Robin said, "All the other mothers spend more time with their daughters," Barbara respond with something to the effect: "Robin, it sounds like you are really frustrated that we don't spend more time together. I really would like it if we could spend more time together as well. However, I need to work to pay the bills. If you get most of your homework done at your after-school program, then when I pick you up we could spend extra time together at the park."

Peter got home from work one Friday afternoon, after his wife Lisa had had a particularly difficult week. It is hard enough to take care of a sick child, but she had been taking care of two sick children that week, when she herself had also been very sick most of the week. Understandably, she was in a bad mood when Peter got home. Peter answered the phone and it was a thoughtful friend of theirs. Peter described how his wife had "ripped his head off" as soon as he got home. Their friend said, "Go put your head back on and help out."

It is important not to take things too personally. It is better to be less defensive and more empathetic. Give people some slack and "go put your head back on."

Can empathy help with the stress of caring for infants and raising young children? When our twins were born we tried to empathize with the newest members of our family. Their crying was not done to annoy us. If their crying was hard to deal with 3:00 a.m. some morning, it was important to reframe the situation and to realize that the crying was our children's only way of communicating their needs. We learned to try one strategy after another until we satisfied their need (feeding? diaper change? sucking? burping? being held? being put down?).

Toddlers are in the process of learning to deal with feelings of anger and frustration. One woman related to an anology of a toddler's feelings during a tantrum as being similar to the worst case of PMS that could be imagined. During tantrums, she tries to keep that analogy in mind to help her empathize with their feelings. She then can better understand that toddlers need help learning to deal with their intense feelings.

Here are some other guidelines for communication:

1. Actively listen — be mindful when you listen and to let go of distracting thoughts. Have you ever spoken to a person who looks past you as you speak and never really hears what you are saying? Perhaps you remember an argument when someone did not hear what you were saying. It's likely you found this type of conversation frustrating. When a learned rabbi was asked his definition of wisdom, he replied that *a wise man knows how to learn from each person he meets.* When you enter into a conversation with someone, learn what that

person feels and thinks. Active, focused listening helps family, work and social relationships. Both people in the conversation benefit from active listening. Even if a goal of the conversation is to present your viewpoint, it will be helpful to understand your communication partner's point of view first.

2. You don't always have to be right. Conversations are less productive when the only objective is to win. Go into a conversation with the objective of learning how the other person feels. Be open to learning information that may change your point of view.

> We must love them both — those whose opinions we share and those whose opinions we reject. For both have labored in the search for truth, and both have helped us in the finding of it.
> ST. THOMAS AQUINAS

Instead of a goal of always being right, have your goal be to effectively communicate. Take pride in your ability to communicate, not in your ability to insist on being right.

3. Instead of criticizing others, try expressing how you feel. In order to do this, you may try using "I" terms instead of "you" terms. When you say "I feel ..." and go on to describe your feelings, people listen and are less likely to get defensive. Also, no one can effectively argue against a statement of how you feel. On the other hand, statements like "You should not have acted that way," and "You were an idiot," are likely to elicit arguments and defensiveness. For example, compare the statements: "You are inconsiderate" with the "I" statement "I was hurt when you insulted me in front of the group." The second statement is more likely to lead to productive communication, instead of a nonproductive argument. (By the way, "I feel that you are an idiot" is not considered an "I" statement. In fact, usually when you say "I feel *that*" instead of "I feel," you are expressing an opinion instead of a feeling.) Consider the following examples:

a. How would you feel if someone were to say to you, "You were inconsiderate for being so late"? Compare that with how you would feel if someone said, "When I didn't hear from you, *I was afraid* that you may have gotten into an accident. I care a lot about you, so please call the next time you are running late."

b. How would you feel if your spouse said, "I can't believe you are eating ice cream again. You know it's not on your diet"? Compare that with, "I really care about you. *I'm afraid* that one day you'll have another heart attack and I might lose you. *It really worries me* when you eat a lot of high-fat foods."

c. How would you feel if someone said: "I feel you are domineering." That statement might sound like a feeling, but it was really an opinion. Compare that with someone expressing the emotion they felt by saying to you: "I *felt hurt* when you did not give me time to express my opinion. I need a moment to let you know what I think about the issue."

4. Both empathy and communicating empathy are essential components of effective communication. Before hearing advice or a lesson in someone else's philosophy, people usually want to be understood. Imagine you have been struggling with a problem. If a friend just quickly volunteers his solution, it might imply to you that he or she does not understand the problem fully and is trivializing your stress. In general, it is best to communicate your understanding of the situation before volunteering advice. Feeling understood can often make someone feel better and more open to a suggestion. Often, feeling understood is all someone needs to feel better.

Sometimes, it is tricky to communicate your understanding. Just saying, "I know how you feel" may lead someone to respond: "How can you know how I feel?" One way to communicate empathy is to paraphrase. Effectively paraphrasing does not mean parroting back what someone said. Rather, paraphrasing means incorporating the key elements of both the content and emotions of what that person said. After a friend tells you a dozen things that went wrong that day, you might express empathy by saying, "It sounds like you had a frustrating day with one problem after another." In another circumstance, you are much better to begin with, "That is a stressful situation," before saying, "Just do _____ to fix the problem."

This strategy is important for talking with both adults and children. One might say to a young child, "That's silly to be upset about losing that stuffed animal; you have several others." Likely, the child would become even more upset that you did not appreciate his or her feelings. Something might not seem important from an adult perspective, but may seem extremely important from the child's perspective. You might do better if you said, "I know you really liked your giraffe. That was upsetting to you to lose it.*

Once in a while, people reach an impasse; neither person understands the other's point of view. Instead of fully listening while the other person is talking, each person spends that time planning how to "win" the conversation. By requiring paraphrasing in this type of conversation, both parties are forced to listen to each other and attempt to empathize.

The following exercise can be used to help two people move beyond an impasse in a conversation: *Only one person is allowed to speak at a time. While this person is making a point he/she holds an object such as a cup. The second person must accurately paraphrase the first person's point before he/she obtains possession of the cup and has a turn to make a point. Not infrequently, it may take a few attempts to accurately paraphrase a point. When the person making the point feels the point was accurately paraphrased the cup changes hands.*

5. Reframing allows you to listen to comments in a constructive, instead of a defensive manner. It also helps in finding a positive meaning in what others say. One woman recounted an interaction with her loving, but sometimes critical, mother. The woman's fiancé had been a successful businessman, but his luck had changed. His business was bankrupt and he also declared personal bankruptcy. When the woman reluctantly revealed the news to her mother, her mother reacted by saying, "You have a knack for finding losers." This statement was very painful for the woman, until she reframed it in a positive light. She reasoned that her mother had meant to convey her

---

*For more information on talking with children, read: *How to Talk So Kids Will Listen & Listen So Kids Will Talk* by Adele Faber and Elaine Mazlish; New York: Avon Books, 1980.

disappointment since she wanted her daughter to find someone successful and to be happy. Once the woman was able to reframe her mother's initial comment and understand its motivation, she felt better.[36] It is not uncommon that apparently negative comments are motivated by caring and concern. Therefore, it often pays to look for the motivation behind a comment.

6. If you are not sure what the other person's point is, ask for clarification. Communication can be improved by asking for clarification not only on a specific statement, but also about associated thoughts and feelings.

7. When someone expresses his or her viewpoint in an emotional or loud manner, there is a tendency to react by becoming argumentative. Instead of immediately getting argumentative or defensive, take a moment to listen to not only the words, but also consider the emotions implied and expressed. Remember that the intensity of the emotion is a loud signal that the issue is very important to the person with whom you are speaking. Therefore, take some extra time and patience to listen to what he or she is saying.

8. If at all possible, avoid saying something that could be interpreted as a threat. Most people (probably like yourself) tend to respond negatively to this form of communication. Just imagine your response if someone said, "Do this, or else."

9. Do not throw in the kitchen sink. That is, keep to the topic of the current disagreement.

10. Keep an internal locus of control. Do not blame others for your emotions. Your conversation will be more productive if you avoid blame in general. Using "I" statements can help you do this.

11. Usually, it is best to address a concern as soon as you can. However, there are times when someone is not available to communicate when you are thinking about a particular issue or you need time to compile your thoughts. When you find yourself reviewing a conversation again and again in your head, list the main points of the conversation on paper. This allows you to more easily quiet your mind since you may feel less of a need to continually rehearse the conversation in your head.

To keep your marriage brimming
With love in the marriage cup,
Whenever you're wrong, admit it
Whenever you're right, shut up.
OGDEN NASH

It probably would not hurt to repeat this poem once a day. This last quote is a humorous way of making the point that it is not wise to communicate with the sole goal of proving you are right. One of the most important mesages in this chapter is to remind yourself to pause when you find yourself in this trap. Aim to fully understand the other person's viewpoint and communicate effectively. Do not take pride in always being right. Take pride in being a good listener and an effective communicator.

Denise had a difficult time getting along with her sister Alice. I asked for a specific example of one of their conversations:

Denise: "I was really hurt when you called me fat in front of other people."

Alice: "You always say things like that to me."

Denise: "I would never do that. You are so inconsiderate."

And then an argument and hard feelings would ensue.

Suggestion of an alternative response for Denise:
"I didn't realize that I did something that hurt you. If you see that I am doing something like that, let me know right away. I really will try my best not to offend you. I care about you and hurting you is the last thing that I would want."

With this alternative response, Denise does not use "you" terms and she does not insist on winning an argument.

Providing Feedback

Everyone wants to be appreciated, so if you appreciate someone,
don't keep it a secret.
MARY KAY ASH
FOUNDER, MARY KAY COSMETICS

Feeling gratitude and not expressing it
is like wrapping a present and not giving it.
WILLIAM ARTHUR WARD

It is helpful to learn to accept other people's behavior. However, some-times it is useful to attempt to change another's behavior by giving effective feedback. Positive feedback is given to make it more likely someone will repeat a desired behavior. In contrast, negative feedback is given to make it less likely that someone will repeat an undesired behavior. Poorly delivered feedback can backfire by making people defensive.

- *Feedback should not be insulting or demeaning.* Demeaning feedback produces defensiveness and hostility instead of the desired results.
- *Feedback should refer to a person's behavior rather than a trait.* For instance, instead of, "You are clumsy," effective feedback might sound like: "When you use the large drill, be sure to use both hands and use the left hand for the lever." Similarly, calling someone "rude" will usually be less effective than asking them to let you finish a story before interrupting.
- *Feedback should be as specific as possible.* Instead of saying "You do careless work," you could explain which specific work project needed improvement and what specific improvements were needed. This precise information will be much more useful to prevent a similar mistake happening in the future.
- *Feedback also needs to be understandable.* Often it is best to avoid jargon and technical terms.

- ***Feedback should be well-timed.*** In general, negative feedback should be given individually, whereas sometimes it is appropriate to give positive feedback in front of a group. Feedback should usually be given as soon after the event as possible. Most of us have assumed that we were doing a task well, but then long after the task was complete, we received some negative feedback. By that time, it was too late to make any changes, but not too late to be annoyed. Therefore, it is helpful for supervisors to frequently give feedback. There is an art however to determining the frequency of feedback. There is the old expression, "Pick your fights." Continuous negative feedback or nit-picking can backfire by having people ignore the important feedback.

- No one likes to hear feedback only when things go wrong. A good hint for giving feedback, whether it be in raising children or talking to coworkers, is to ***catch someone doing something right. Positive feedback can be as effective, or even more effective, than negative feedback.*** Positive feedback has an added bonus — the next time negative feedback is given, it is likely to be received more willingly and less defensively. When we are working hard, no one likes to hear only negative comments. All of the preceding points about feedback are applicable to positive as well as negative feedback. "You are conscientious" is a nice compliment. Compliments definitely have their place. However, telling someone the specific behavior you liked in understandable terms will more likely increase the chances that he or she will continue the behavior.

Many people do not offer feedback according to the guidelines outlined above. However, even poorly delivered feedback may contain a message worth considering. There is skill in receiving feedback, as well as giving it. If someone offers feedback to you that is not specific or is about a trait rather than a behavior, it is tempting to get defensive and perhaps even angry. ***Before reacting with anger, consider asking for clarification. Is there a specific behavior that should be improved?*** Instead of getting defensive, you can then ascertain if there is useful advice that can be garnered from the feedback.

Ann was getting frustrated with a coworker, Robin. At most of their group meetings, it seemed like Robin would "nit-pick" about Ann's performance. This was incredibly stressful for Ann. On my suggestion, Ann reframed the situation and realized that Robin, at times, actually had some useful feedback. When Ann thought about it, she realized that what she really resented was that the feedback was given in a group setting. Instead of being angry at Robin, she thanked Robin for the feedback that was useful. She then requested that the feedback be given privately. Thereafter, Ann and Robin got along better and Ann could actually use some of Robin's feedback, instead of just growing annoyed at her "nit-picking."

Wendy was very frustrated about the performance of her employees. She felt like she would ask them to do a task and it would often be done incorrectly. I asked if she had checked with her employees to see why they were not getting the job done. She said that she had asked. However, what she had asked was, "Did you not listen to me, or are you just not able to do the job?" I asked Wendy to consider checking into the problem in a way that would be less demeaning to her employees. I emphasized with Wendy that it was more important to effectively communicate than to try to "be right." She had more success when she said, "It seems I am not effectively communicating what needs to be done. Is there a different or new way that I could discuss the assignment, so you understand it better?" Once she did give the instructions, she could check if her employee understood them. For instance, she could say, "I'm still not sure I am doing a good job getting my message across. This information might be confusing. To make sure I did get the message across, could you please tell me your understanding of what we discussed, before you get started on the project?"

Assertiveness

A "no" uttered from the deepest conviction is better and greater
than a "yes" merely uttered to please, or what is worse, to avoid trouble.
MAHATMA GANDHI

Assertiveness is an important communication skill and a useful tool in dealing with stress. For our purposes, assertiveness means expressing your desires. It does not mean being aggressive, obnoxious or rude. Assertiveness often takes the form of saying "no" when you don't want to do something. Overextending ourselves can easily lead to higher stress. Even when we do not overextend ourselves, the preoccupation with what others think causes us much stress. It is important not to invest too much energy in worrying about what other people think of us. Let these excessive thoughts go and do what you know to be right. As Shakespeare said, "To thine own self be true." Mahatma Gandhi said, "Happiness is when what you think, what you say, and what you do are in harmony." It is more important to follow your own sense of integrity and morality than it is to win others' approval.

Henry was performing well at work, but he found himself increasingly busy and stressed. As soon as he finished one project, he was assigned two more. Before he knew it, he was working 70 to 80 hours a week and other areas of his life were suffering. He came to me complaining of palpitations and anxiety. Henry finally realized that it was rare to find a boss who would start a conversation by saying, "Take it easy; you've worked too hard already." When Henry voiced his desires in a polite, yet assertive, way, his boss was more than willing to accommodate Henry's request for a decreased work load. The palpitations improved and Henry had the chance to develop other parts of his life – including a new relationship.

Let's look at the above example more closely. Henry had several options:

1. Give in and accept any added work his boss would give him (passive response)
2. Angrily call his boss inconsiderate (aggressive response).
3. Politely, yet firmly advise his boss that his "plate was already full" with other tasks (assertive response). Notice how each of these assertive responses might be an appropriate response, so Henry could have some time off work:
   - "I'm already busy with two other projects, so I don't think that I'll have time for the new project."
   - "I'm doing the Smith and Jones project now and I need to be home by 6 p.m. tonight. If you would like me to work on the new project, I'll have to postpone the others. Which project would you prefer that I complete today?"

We cannot count on a boss, coworker, or spouse to automatically try to decrease our stress load. It is essential to realize that, if we don't speak up for ourselves, often no one will.

The Clerk is Not a Jerk

I remember, many years ago, reading a book that espoused the saying "the clerk is a jerk." What the author meant was that if you want to get something of value from a store, like a refund, you should seek the manager and not just settle for a negative response from a store salesperson or clerk. It may be true that if you do not get satisfaction from a salesperson, talking with the manager will be helpful. However, far too often people do not treat staff members at a place of business with respect. As the saying goes, "You catch a lot more flies with honey than with vinegar."

When you deal with people with respect and with a caring attitude, you will accomplish much more and both of the parties involved will be less frustrated. You can always ask to speak to a supervisor later, but you may surprise yourself at what can be accomplished by being pleasant and non-threatening to other employees first.

Keep this in mind, too, when talking to people on the phone. It is often too easy to forget that there is another real person on the other end of the line.

Summary

Throughout this chapter, we have discussed a variety of communication skills. By effectively implementing these skills, your relationships with people will improve in all aspects of your life. By practicing acceptance, empathy, genuiness and assertiveness, your life will become less stressful and more fulfilled.

---

[35] Rogers, Carl. *A Way of Being*. Boston: Houghton Mifflin Company, 1980, pp. 22–23.

[36] Adapted from a story by mediator Judith Rubenstein.

10

Manage Anger and Frustration

Holding onto anger is like holding on to a hot coal
with the intent of throwing it at someone else;
you are the one that gets burned.

BUDDHA

If we could read the secret history of our enemies,
we should find in each man's life sorrow and
suffering enough to disarm all hostility.

LONGFELLOW

Anger, hostility, irritation, impatience and frustration are emotions that certainly increase our level of distress. Researchers show that the anger and hostility are probably bigger risk factors for heart disease than are the other components of Type A behavior.[37]

The country of Tibet was invaded by China in 1949. By some estimates, six thousand Tibetan temples were destroyed and a million Tibetans died as a result of Chinese occupation. The Dalai Lama is the spiritual leader of the Tibetan Buddhists. "When asked about his apparent lack of anger toward the Chinese ... the Dalai Lama replied something to the effect that: 'They have taken everything from us; should I let them take my mind as well?'"[38] The Dalai Lama realized that if he were to harbor anger and resentment for the Chinese, he, not the Chinese, would be the one to give up peace of mind. The Dalai Lama continues to work toward his goal of a free Tibet, but without anger dominating his mind.

How do we deal with our anger? One of the most effective ways to decrease anger is through empathy. If you are angry with someone, try your best to put yourself in that other person's shoes. Perhaps you might not imagine acting the way another person acted, but you might be able to understand his or her motivation. You might be able to empathize with the frustration, anger, despair, or misunderstanding that leads another to act in a certain manner.

Next time you start fuming about the guy who cut you off on the freeway, remember a time when you mistakenly took another's right of way. When you get annoyed with someone, do your best to try to imagine what it would be like to be in their position. It's important to remember that when people are rude, they are usually suffering in one way or another.

> The weak can never forgive. Forgiveness is the attribute of the strong.
> *MAHATMA GANDHI*

Another way to deal with anger is through forgiveness. Our families and friends are too important to us for us to continue harboring resentment. If you hold a grudge, it negatively affects your psychological well-being. We have all acted inappropriately at one time or another. We also have had people treat us inappropriately. They may have said or done something that was really off base. Being able to forgive is one of the most important acts we can do for our relationships and our health.

The Berenstain Bears is a collection of wonderful children's books. Sometimes children's books have lessons for adults as well. In *The Berenstain Bears Get in a Fight*, Mama Bear tries to help Brother and Sister Bear to make up after their fight:

> "Everybody gets in an argument once in a while," she said. "Even folks who love each other very much... We get angry, even call each other names and say things we really don't mean — and after a while it's over." "Like the storm?" asked Sister... "Yes," said Mama. "Like the storm." "Look!" said Papa.

The sun shining on the last of the rain had made a rainbow. "A rainbow is something very beautiful that happens after a storm," said Mama... "You mean like making up after a big fight?" "Sort of," said Mama.[39]

I clearly remember times in my life when I was angry and said something I should not have — something I did not mean that was upsetting to another. I can also think of misunderstandings when someone else said something I found very rude and offensive. My initial inclination was not to just let bygones-be-bygones. My first instinct was to hold a grudge — a really good grudge. I recall when I was annoyed enough with someone's outburst that it really had the potential to ruin a whole family vacation. That is when it pays to remember the analogy of an argument with a storm. In anger, we make statements we do not mean, but when it is over it is over. Forgiveness and "making up" might be even more beautiful than a rainbow. Our families, friends, coworkers and the rest of the world could use a good, healthy dose of forgiveness.

There are also meditative approaches to dealing with anger. Sometimes we obsess about an incident until we get angrier and angrier. Every time we tell the story and blame someone else for our anger, it is as if we are pouring oil on the flames of our anger. If left to its own devices, anger behaves more like a bouncing tennis ball. Anger over an event may return repeatedly, but each time it comes up, the intensity of the anger decreases, like the tennis ball that bounces lower each time. Finally, the energy is dissipated. When you stop blaming others for your emotions, and just notice the physical sensations and thoughts associated with anger, the anger will more quickly dissipate. If you feel a knot in your stomach it might be helpful to meditate using the mantra: "Breathing in, I notice tightness in my abdomen ... breathing out, I ease the tension in my abdomen." If you are too upset to sit still, consider a walking meditation. (Note: this technique is for temporary mild discomfort associated with anger. For severe pain, please consult your physician.)

It is important not to just sit there and let your anger stew to a point that it eventually explodes. The above guidelines will help you with this.

Additionally, it is helpful to address the circumstances surrounding the anger. In other words, communicate your feelings and address the situation before you get extremely upset. Be mindful of the assertiveness and feedback skills discussed in this chapter. If, for some reason, you cannot communicate about the problem right away, writing the issues down can be helpful. It can help by decreasing the likelihood you will repeat the thoughts again and again, since you know the points are already on paper. Also, you have the opportunity to think about how you want to communicate effectively, instead of just reacting in a way that could inflame the situation.

Another way to deal with anger is to reframe a situation. As discussed in Chapter 4, when you encounter someone who is rude, instead of dwelling on how terrible he/she is, consider how that person is probably suffering in one way or another.

One of the most popular television shows of 2000 was "Survivor." Toward the end of the game, one of the contestants voiced her feelings about another contestant. One participant told another that if she were dying of thirst in the desert, she would rather see her die and be eaten by vultures than give her a drop of water. THIS WAS ABOUT A GAME! This degree of hatred should be reserved for a mass murderer, such as Hitler. How often do we overreact? I have seen people unleash a torrent of anger about a relatively small matter. Does the person you are angry with deserve such hostility? Is that person so evil?

In *The Art of Happiness,* the Dalai Lama describes other ways of deal-ing with anger.[40] When people "fall in love," they tend to see only the pos-itive traits in the other person. In a similar way, when we become angry with someone, we only think of that person's negative traits. By deliber-ately listing that person's positive traits, we can decrease the anger. Your boss may be very stern, but what good qualities does he/she possess.

The Dalai Lama also stresses the importance of learning the skill of patience. He reminds us that people who frustrate us, or even wish us ill, are also the ones that give us the opportunity to learn the vital skill of patience.

A final way to deal with anger is to channel the feelings in a produc-tive fashion. That is, use the feelings to benefit your own and/or another's well-being. Bob woke up at 3:00 a.m. one morning, craving a cigarette. This was 19 years ago — before there was an abundance of 24-hour mar-kets. He thought about going to a market 20 miles away to get a pack of cigarettes. When he realized the hold cigarettes had on him, he got so angry it gave him the strength to quit smoking.

There must be few experiences in life that are more emotionally difficult than a parent dealing with the death of a young child. How can a parent deal with the anger of a child's life ended prematurely? In several instances, parents have done something productive with that anger. For instance, many children have died from improperly secured child safety seats. Parents of one of these children helped to publicize the prevalence and seriousness of this problem. By doing so, they saved many young lives. By using anger productively and nonviolently, we can have the potential to create changes like these and also work against a variety of societal injustices (as was done in the civil rights movement).

———

I feel incredibly blessed to have my two wonderful sons. They have given me immeasurable joy. At the end of a day, when I am alone, supervising my twin two-year-old boys, there have certainly been times of frustration as well.

For instance, putting on sunscreen might not seem like a very difficult task. However, when this involves two-year-old twins, who either do not want sunscreen or want to do the whole application on their own, the task can certainly become more challenging.

During one such episode with the boys, I noticed my frustration starting to increase. I thought about the typical process of how we make anger worse and hold on to anger. We might feel physical sensations like tightness in our abdomen or jaw. These sensations are typically followed by thoughts like: "I am angry," or "I am really frustrated." Since anger and frustration are often considered negative emotions, we often justify the emotions to ourselves. We tell ourselves the story we feel both created and justified the anger. Each time we tell the story we get more and more angry (or more and more frustrated). Instead, by just accepting our feelings, and not being compelled to

*repeatedly justify them, we give the anger or frustration
the opportunity to quickly dissipate.*

*Before my frustration had a chance to build, I took some
diaphragmatic breaths and chuckled. I realized that my
twins were two wonderful teachers. By learning skills to
patiently watch two active boys, I would have skills that I
could use in many other areas of my life.*

*Since then, before I get too frustrated, I catch myself
and think of my two wonderful little teachers, enjoy a nice
breath and laugh. Of course, when I once said something
out loud about my two little teachers, they said, "Dad, we
are not little teachers; we are big boys!"*

*When I find myself frustrated in other situations, thinking
of people as my teachers can bring a little smile to my face
and a little creativity in trying to deal with a situation.*

---

[37] Braunwald, Eugene M.D. (editor); *Heart Disease: A Textbook of Cardiovascular Medicine,* 16th ed; New York: W. B. Saunders Company, 2001; pp. 2244–2245.

[38] Kabat-Zinn, Jon. *Wherever You Go There You Are.* New York: Hyperion, 1994. p. 49.

[39] Berenstain, Stan and Jan, *The Berenstain Bears Get in a Fight,* New York: Random House, 1982.

[40] The Dalai Lama and Howard C. Cutler, M.D. *The Art of Happiness,* New York: Riverhead Books, 1998. Ch. 10.

11

∽

Take the Stress Out of Decisions

When you come to a fork in the road, take it.

YOGI BERRA

Half the worry in the world is caused by people trying to make decisions before they have sufficient knowledge on which to base a decision.

DEAN HAWKES

For some of us, the times of greatest stress involve making decisions. We need to make many decisions throughout the day — some big, and some small. It seems that, as our society becomes more advanced, the number of decisions we must make increases. The decisions range from what kind of toothpaste to buy to where we are going to live or work. There are several ideas that we can keep in mind to help ease some of the stress involved with decision-making:

1. As the Dean Hawkes' quote implies, *doing the necessary research* is important. For instance, there may be important information in a book or on the Internet that could help with your decision. Ultimately, the decision may be yours, but seeking the advice of others or discussing the options with others can be helpful. Seek someone who is an expert in the field or someone who has had to make a similar decision. You can discuss the decision with other people

that will be affected by its outcome. Some of the people to consider consulting include your family, friends, coworkers, counselor, clergy, or doctor.

2. Remind yourself that *most decisions are not permanent.* If you try something out and you don't like it, you can usually change your mind. It may be inconvenient to change your mind, and in some cases, not possible. Keep in mind, however, that many decisions are not final.

3. Remember the concept of *internal locus of control.* Keep in mind that our happiness and peace of mind will be most influenced by internal factors such as our attitudes, and our willingness to focus on the present. We probably can be happy or sad whether we live in Kansas or California, or whether we go to one college or another. We can frequently view our decisions as two alternatives we could be happy with, as opposed to thinking that all of our happiness depends on the right decision.

4. *If a decision is hard to make, it implies that both choices compare closely in their virtues.* That is, if one choice were much better than the other, the decision would be easy.

5. Asking yourself, "Will this decision *matter in 10 years?*" will put certain decisions in perspective. The answer, often, is that it will not matter. If it will, keep the other suggestions in mind.

6. Make a *pro's and con's list.* Sometimes decision-making is easier when the advantages and disadvantages of each course of action is on paper. Having the issues on paper will also decrease the tendency to argue the points over and over in your head.

7. At times, the best course of action is *sitting with or sleeping on a decision,* rather than worrying. Have you ever struggled with a decision, and then suddenly, something happens or an idea occurs to you, and the best choice becomes clear? This is a common phenomenon. If a decision needs to be made now, you should not procrastinate. However, frequently there is time available to consider the options. Instead of spending this time worrying, acknowledge that certain choices may become clearer on their own with a little time.

8. In times of extreme emotional turmoil, it may be best, if possible, to postpone important decisions. For instance, when faced with the recent loss of a loved one, it may be difficult to rationally weigh the pros and cons of a complicated decision.

9. *Brainstorming* on your own or with another person can be helpful. If you have two obvious choices, with some brainstorming you'll likely have additional choices. The first step is to come up with as many options as you can, no matter how impractical they might seem. You may ask a friend or group of friends, coworkers or an organization to help. Later, you can critically analyze each choice to come up with a smaller, more practical list that may include more than the initial two options.

10. Focusing on the *values* involved in the decision and then weighing those values can be helpful. For instance, some decisions may involve the choice of a job with a higher salary versus another that pays less, but that you might find more fulfilling in other ways. In considering the 40 or more hours per week you may be at your job, a more fulfilling job may be more important. However, if earning less means more difficulty actually putting food on the table, the additional fulfillment might not be as important.

11. The importance of *integrity* cannot be overemphasized. Don't waste your time feeling guilty. To quote Abraham Lincoln: "When I do good, I feel good. When I do bad, I feel bad. That's my religion." Make the decision you can be proud of and feel good about it. With certain decisions, you simply know what is right. Do it. Think about what your guiding principles are. For example, "Do not do any harm and if possible try to help others." If you are religious, consider what you think God would want you to do. Alternatively, you might ask yourself, "What course of action would I be proud to discuss with my children?"

12. Sometimes a decision is more difficult when there is a lot of static in our minds. If your mind seems to be racing, *meditate, take a walk, or practice a walking meditation.* These activities may help clear your mind and enable you to make a better decision.

———————

Fred had another strategy for dealing with business decisions. At times, two people would offer him a deal and he could only accept one of the offers. He found that letting both parties know when the decision was close could often help him make the decision. One of the parties would frequently go that extra mile for the business deal.

David was in his 60's and was a retired business owner. He was getting "attacks" that he thought might be seizures. With one episode, he was driving and his wife called him on the cell phone. He started talking on the phone and realized that, as he exited the freeway, he had forgotten to slow down. He had to tell himself to lift his leg up from the gas and put it on the brake. He got the car to stop by the time he got to the stop sign. He then drove off and realized that the cell phone was on his lap. He put it to his ear and his wife was still talking. She had not known anything had happened. He wondered if the episode was a seizure. I told him I did not think he was having seizures at all. He had simply been distracted by talking on the cell phone and it would be safer for him not to talk on the cell phone as he drove or, at the minimum, use a "hands-free device."

But David was still worried. He said that similar episodes occurred when he had been excited or stressed. On further exploration, he said that it felt like he had so many thoughts occurring, he was overwhelmed and "paralyzed." However, if he were in a conversation at the time, no one would even notice his problem.

David admitted he was under a lot of stress. Now that he had retired, he felt that he was wasting his life. He knew that he would not live forever and felt that he was not living up to his potential; he did not feel productive. When I asked what he would want to do, he said he thought about spending a year traveling around Europe.

His wife, however, still worked and liked her job very much. She did not want to leave on a year-long trip. He wondered aloud about spending a year away from her and it was causing a lot of arguments.

David wanted to decide what he should do with his time. To help him with that decision, I asked him to clarify his values. I asked him to just brainstorm and list all his important values. After he completed the list, I asked him to put the values in order of importance. Number one on the list was his and his wife's happiness. Also high on the list was being productive and spending time with friends. He realized that spending a year traveling by himself in Europe would not make his wife happy, would take him away from his friends, and would not necessarily make him feel productive. And as far as making himelf happy, David admitted that he had once come home early from a four-day trip, largely because he had missed his wife. After David reviewed his important values, he realized that the year in Europe by himself was not the way to go. What should he do? I asked that he give himself a few weeks to sit with that decision.

Also on David's list of values was keeping busy. He had always liked to be active. In fact, he said that he avoided solitary activities such as going by himself for a quiet walk on the beach. In times like that, he would predictably become sad. Therefore, he always wanted to be busy.

My next suggestion for David was to practice those quiet, still times. Take quiet walks, and just notice his breath. I asked him to be with the sadness and notice how it just passes when he stops running from it. Learn to enjoy the stillness, the breath, the sun, the breeze, a sunset, the soft sand on his feet.... Once David did not have to run from the stillness, he could find a balance in his life. At times, he then could enjoy a busy life, but not feel compelled to do so; at other times, he could enjoy some peacefulness.

David also considered other options for how to spend his time. He did not need extra money, so his options included not only regular employment, but also finding some meaningful volunteer work. There was not an immediate deadline for his decision. As opposed to struggling with his decision, David sat with the decision — trusting that the right answer would come to him. Not much later, he was called with a fascinating consulting opportunity close to home. Still, he always wanted to travel to places like China. However, now David realized that a month-long vacation, in which his wife could accompany him, suited his needs much better than a year-long trip.

12

⸎

Improve Your Sleep

People who say they sleep like a baby usually don't have one.

LEO J. BURKE

Stress and sleep have an interesting relationship. A good night's sleep is very beneficial for handling stress. However, when people are very stressed, they often have trouble sleeping. How much sleep do you need? The simple answer is, you need enough sleep to feel rested. For some people, that can mean five hours and, for other people it can mean ten hours. In general, people tend to need less sleep as they age.

A research study in March 1999 compared several insomnia treatments for people over 65. One group received one of the most popularly prescribed sleeping pills (temazepam; brand name, Restoril™). A second group was given recommendations for changing behavior at bedtime, while a third group received both the behavioral recommendations and the medication, and the final group only received a placebo. The only groups with long-term benefit were the groups that were given the behavioral treatments.[41]

If you are having trouble getting to sleep, consider some of these hints:

1. Avoid caffeine in the afternoon or evening. Caffeine can be found in coffee, chocolate, many sodas, and caffeinated teas. Certain medications, like decongestants, can cause insomnia for some people.

(Speak with your doctor about other options for treating nasal congestion, if needed.) Alcohol sometimes helps with getting to sleep initially, but it may interfere with the quality of sleep and make it more likely that you will awaken in the middle of the night.

2.   Avoid heavy meals right before bedtime.

3.   Regular exercise is important and can help with sleep. However, it is best to avoid exercise in the two hours just before bed.

4.   Use the bedroom only for sleep and sex. Avoid eating, doing work activities, or talking on the phone in bed. It is helpful to have your body associate your bedroom with sleep.

5.   A regular evening routine such as taking a warm bath, meditating, or another relaxing activity can help with sleep.

6.   Make your bedroom dark, quiet, and a comfortable temperature.

7.   If you tend to worry a lot, write your concerns on paper. This can help prevent you from thinking about your problems again and again at night.

8.   Perhaps most importantly, don't try too hard. If you try to go to sleep for 30 minutes and feel like you are struggling, get up from bed and do something else. It's useful to have a boring book on hand — something that you can get up and read (perhaps with a glass of warm skim milk) until you feel tired. Then go back to bed. Of course, one of the keys is picking a boring book, not a suspense novel.

9.   Try waking up and going to sleep at the same time every day. This can help your body establish a rhythm.

10.   If you are having trouble sleeping, try a relaxation exercise. An example of such an exercise is included on Track 4 of CD 2. It includes a guided meditation and some guided imagery. When using this CD as a sleep aid, set the volume relatively low. Plan to listen to this meditation, and if you are still awake, spend another 20 minutes in quiet relaxation. If you are still having trouble sleeping, then go to your boring book and warm glass of milk.

11.   If you continue to have problems with regular insomnia, contact your doctor.

Almost everyone has trouble sleeping on occasion. However, if insomnia occurs frequently and does not improve with the above suggestions, you may want to discuss it with your doctor. Insomnia can sometimes be caused by medical problems. For instance, an enlarged prostate can cause a man to wake up frequently to urinate. Awakening with shortness of breath is a definite reason to seek a doctor's advice. Clinical depression and anxiety disorders can also cause insomnia and are described in Chapter 14.

With sleep apnea, people may stop breathing for over 20 seconds at a time. This awakens them long enough to get a breath. People with sleep apnea can wake up over one hundred times in a night without being aware of it. Obviously, this can cause considerable fatigue. They may get morning headaches and high blood pressure as well. Usually, but not always, people with sleep apnea are overweight and loud snorers. Additionally, untreated sleep apnea increases the risk of heart disease, so it is important for people with this problem to seek medical attention.

Restless leg syndrome is another cause of insomnia. When people with this problem go to bed, their legs involuntarily kick and move. This can wake up both themselves and their partners. Several medications are useful in treating restless leg syndrome.

---

[41] Morin C. et al, "Behavioral and pharmacological therapies for late-life insomnia: A randomized controlled trial," *Journal of the American Medical Association.* March 19, 1999; Vol 281: 991–999.

13

Combining Strategies

The whole is more than
the sum of its parts.

ARISTOTLE

T hroughout this book so far, we have discussed multiple strategies for
dealing with stress. In our busy lives might there be ways to combine
these different strategies to make even more efficient use of our time
and perhaps make them even more effective for dealing with our stress?

For instance, a regular practice of sitting meditation can be extremely
effective in both dealing with current stress and also in learning mindfulness. Regular exercise is also an important part of a healthy lifestyle
and, in its own right, a very effective way to deal with stress. If we do a
walking meditation, it can be combined with both of these important
activities. As you walk or jog, enjoy breathing the air, and observe the
sights and sounds in the environment. Consider doing a mantra that
might consist of just counting "1, 2, 3, 4" with the inhalation and "1, 2,
3, 4" with the exhalation. Other options are to say something like "peace"
with the in-breath and "love" or "smile" with the out-breath. If your
thoughts drift, gently bring them back to the mantra.

After anywhere from 5 to 20 minutes of following your mantra or
breath, you can move to the next step of thinking about events and people for which you are grateful. As you stand tall, think to yourself something like,"I am so grateful to have my son, Leo, in my life." Say it with

conviction and visualize your child's face as you do this. Be grateful for what is directly around you in this present moment. You might say, "Thank you, God for my ability to hear the birds singing." If you cannot hear, you might say, "I feel very privileged to feel the wind or sun on my face." Some of the other areas for which you can express gratitude may include your basic necessities (like food and shelter), family, friends, work, health, or hobbies.

After 5 to 20 minutes devoted to gratefulness, you may want to start visualizing your plans for the day. Imagine how you will make your day go well. What might be exciting about the day? What challenges might the day bring? Visualize how you can meet those challenges. We do not have total control over our entire external environment. Situations may go as we plan or they might not. If something does not go as planned, resolve to learn from the process and not think of it as a failure. Visualize how you might use some of your stress management or communication techniques to confidently deal with any challenge that might happen today. At the end of the exercise, again note just a few things for which you are grateful and congratulate yourself for setting aside time for yourself and your body.

Anthony Robbins makes this time for exercise and gratitude a backbone of his *Get the Edge* audio course.[42] In addition, he asks people to reflect on magical or special moments and also to repeat positive phrases out loud such as, "All I need is within me now."

In summary: do the walking or running meditation, spend some time on gratitude, and then visualize the day. This type of combination can be used with other types of exercise, such as swimming. If you do this exercise first thing in the morning every (or most) mornings, it will make an enormous difference in your life.

My life had become very busy. I had twin boys and a busy practice. For some time, both my exercise regime and sleep patterns suffered. I had started drinking two or three mugs of coffee per day in order to compensate. In the long run, it seemed like a vicious cycle. The coffee would help temporarily, but after the caffeine wore off, I sometimes felt worse and drank another cup. I resolved to wake up earlier in the morning (before the rest of the family was awake) and do a 25-minute run.

During the run, I would usually start meditating, then think about the things for which I was grateful, and then visualize how I could enjoy my day. I was really enjoying the routine. When I started the morning running routine, I stopped drinking the coffee and actually felt much more energetic, even when I did not get many hours of sleep. Interestingly, I found that improving my posture by standing up straighter seemed to improve my energy level as well. I remembered my earlier injuries, so I avoided the mistake of starting with a five-mile run, and instead kept with a shorter distance. Once in a while, I might swim instead, to give my legs a rest. In the meantime, I avoided evening television, so that I might get to bed earlier. In order to facilitate the early morning jog, I would get everything ready the night before. I might even wear my jogging shorts and a T-shirt to bed. I would try to iron my shirt and get my work clothes ready the night before, knowing that time in the morning may be tight.

I was really enjoying my time alone to run, meditate, and be grateful. Believe it or not, when I went to sleep, I would even look forward to this time. One morning, the rest of my family woke up early and my wife said, "Boys, how about a run with Dad?" So much for that time alone. However, flexibility is important. Not only did we have a great run with the baby jogger, but I still got my gratitude time ... only it was better. I could share it with my sons. We talked together about all the things in life for which we were grateful. Not only did I focus my attention on gratitude, but hopefully I helped instill a great habit for my

> *sons. Sometimes I run on my own and sometimes with the*
> *boys. Either way, it is great (although running up a steep*
> *hill with two boys in a baby jogger is not a cake walk).*

The next combination is especially useful for intimate/sexual relationships. Pamela Madison, founder of the Women's Sexuality Center in Santa Barbara, discusses a practice called "daily devotions."* If you do not water your garden, the plants will likely die. If you do not nourish your sexual relationship, it may also suffer. We need to make time for each other, and that may be difficult in a family with multiple work and child-rearing commitments.

During your daily devotions, you make 5 to 10 minutes of time together twice-a-day a priority. This time is usually not for sexual intercourse to orgasm, but rather a time to connect. Often there is a difference in libidos (sex drives) in a marriage. Making it clear that there is no expectation of orgasm during these sessions may make the partner with a lesser libido more willing to participate and not to feel pressured.

During these sessions, the couple can try meditating together. One way is to focus on breathing together or on taking alternate breaths (as one partner inhales the other exhales and vise versa). The couple may then want to bring gratitude to the practice. Tell your partner what qualities in him or her you really appreciate both physically, emotionally and spiritually. Sexual play can often be part of the session; however, the goal is not orgasm.

One traditional posture for this is called "Yab-Yum." This might or might not be comfortable for a particular couple. For a heterosexual couple, the male sits cross-legged on the floor, bed or pillow and the female sits facing him with her legs wrapped around him. Additional pillows may help with this posture. Whatever posture, make it comfortable and have fun. Do not take yourself too seriously. Have some time to laugh.

Setting aside longer times for sex is important for most relationships as well. Do not wait to be in the mood for your daily devotions or for your

---

*The Women's Sexuality Center web site is www.womensexualitycenter.

longer dates. Know that this time is essential for you and your partner's emotional and spiritual health.

With the longer sessions, orgasms will be more likely. However, even with the longer sessions, making the orgasm a goal can be counterproductive. If the goal is connection, both male and female orgasms are probably more likely and the journey to get there can be much more enjoyable.

When the marriage is well-nourished, the whole family benefits. Depending on your children's ages, you may need to set aside some time when your children are asleep or, if they are older, they might be able to play without you during the 5 to 10 minute daily devotional. Perhaps once a week you might arrange baby-sitting or opt to take turns watching another family's children in order to spend perhaps two hours once-a-week for a longer period of intimacy.*

> Don't wait to be in the mood to make love.
> Instead, make love to create the mood.
> *PAMELA MADISON*

These two combinations have the potential to improve your life. Making time everyday for an exercise/meditation/gratitude exercise can make a huge difference in how you feel. If you are in an intimate relationship, the daily devotions can significantly improve how you relate as a couple, and how you feel about your relationship.

---

*If you are having problems with sexual function, your family doctor can be a good source of information (either for medication or counselling referrals). Whenever there is a long pause during an office visit with a male patient, I know what the likely subject will be. Problems with sexual function are extremely common. Otherwise, Viagra™ would not be a billion-dollar-drug.

---

[42] Robbins, Anthony. *Get the Edge*. San Diego: Robbins Research International, Inc. (available at www.gettheedge.com)2000

14

∞∞∞

When It's More than Stress

He that won't be counseled can't be helped.

BENJAMIN FRANKLIN

One evening in the early 1980s, I was talking with a friend in a smoky bar. Suddenly, I felt an anxious urge to leave. At that time, I interpreted the feelings as claustrophobia. Several years later, I was in a house with a lot of animals, and noticed similar feelings. My chest felt "tight," and it was difficult to breathe. My lung function was tested, and sure enough, it was significantly abnormal. I had asthma. That's likely what the tight anxious feeling had been years earlier.

Although the medical conditions I will describe in this chapter are not the most common causes of anxiety, neither are they rare. One of the more frequent examples of a medical problem causing anxiety is hyperthyroidism; typical symptoms include a racing heart beat, weight loss, anxiety, and feeling excessively warm. Other signs of hyperthyroidism may include bulging of the eyes, enlargement of the thyroid gland (located in the front part of the neck), and an increase in the resting pulse rate.

In contrast to hyperthyroidism, where the thyroid hormone level is high, hypothyroidism is a condition in which the thyroid hormone level is low. This problem tends to be associated with weight gain instead of weight loss, and it can also be associated with depression. I recently saw one woman who had been previously diagnosed as having postpartum depression. However, since the incidence of hypothyroidism is relatively high during the months following childbirth, I tested her for this, and, indeed, she did have hypothyroidism. With replacement of the thyroid hormone she felt much better, and the depression resolved.

If palpitations (racing or prominent heartbeat) are the most prevalent symptom of your anxiety, taking your pulse rate during the palpitations and discussing it with your doctor can help clarify the nature of the problem. See, Figures 4 and 5 on page 86 for instructions on taking your pulse. In general, a resting pulse rate between 50 and 100 that is regular in rhythm is not worrisome. An occasional early or late beat is usually not of concern. However, if the pulse is totally irregular or stays above 120 to 130 at rest, immediate medical attention is indicated. A pulse rate that is consistently between 100 and 120 at rest may be the result of anxiety, panic attacks, deconditioning, or hyperthyroidism. If you have chest pain or shortness of breath with the palpitations, seek medical attention immediately.

Alcoholism and drug abuse are also associated with excessive amounts of anxiety. In addition, as we discussed in Chapter 7, caffeine and certain prescription and nonprescription medications can cause anxiety. Common offenders are decongestants, diet pills, and asthma medications. If someone is on medication for diabetes, anxiety can result from the blood sugar going too low. Do not discontinue prescription medications without consulting your health care provider. Abrupt discontinuation of certain medications can also cause temporary anxiety and other more serious problems.

There are a few other extremely rare medical problems, such as noncancerous adrenal tumors that can cause anxiety. Testing for these problems would be necessary only in specific circumstances. (Such circumstances might include when the anxiety is associated with a very high blood pressure, racing heart, headache, and feeling flushed.) Obviously, if the anxiety is associated with a symptom such as severe chest discomfort or shortness of breath, immediate medical attention is indicated.

The Anxiety Disorders

Excessive anxiety is more commonly caused by *anxiety disorders.* In fact, approximately fifteen percent of the people in the United States will have an anxiety disorder at sometime in their lives.[43] We all have stress, but when the anxiety is so severe that it significantly interferes with work or other aspects of your life, it may be considered an anxiety disorder. These medical disorders may be partially or fully a result of a shift in the normal biochemistry of the brain.

There are billions of nerve cells in the brain. Messages are transmitted down the length of an individual nerve cell by very small electrical impulses. Single nerve cells communicate with other nerve cells, through chemical signals called *neurotransmitters.* Altered levels of these neurotransmitters can contribute to anxiety disorders or clinical depression. There are a variety of medications that can help with these disorders by regulating the levels of neurotransmitters. Many of these medications are not addictive. Potentially addictive medications may also be beneficial, when used carefully and with appropriate medical supervision.

People usually accept prescribed medication when they have been diagnosed with diabetes. However, some people with anxiety disorders or depression are reluctant to take medication. In persons with diabetes, the pancreas does not produce sufficient insulin (or the cells are not sensitive to the insulin that is present); with some anxiety disorders or depression the brain does not produce enough of a particular neurotransmitter (or perhaps the nerve cells are not sensitive enough to the amount of neurotransmitter that is present). For many people, non-pharmaceutical stress management techniques work well enough. However, for people with severe anxiety disorders, additional treatments may be needed.

Anxiety disorders and depression are medical conditions. It should not be viewed as weakness to take medication for these problems, any more than it is weakness to take medication for diabetes. Diabetes can be treated with diet and exercise. However, when these changes alone are not effective enough, medication is also needed. In the same way, if the techniques you've read about in this book and/or counseling are not working well enough for an anxiety disorder, medication may be needed. Anxiety disorders fall into many different categories. For each type of disorder there are effective types of medication and counseling.

The burden of mental illness on health and productivity in the United States and throughout the world has long been underestimated. Data developed by the massive *Global Burden of Disease* study conducted by the World Health Organization, the World Bank, and Harvard University, reveal that mental illness, including suicide, accounts for over 15 percent of the burden of disease in established market economies, such as the United States. This is more than the disease burden caused by all cancers.
NATIONAL INSTITUTE OF MENTAL HEALTH

Someone with a severe anxiety disorder can be immobilized with anxiety. The anxiety can make functioning at work or home impossible. Imagine you're driving along the freeway. Suddenly your heart starts racing, you feel like you can't breathe, you are shaking, your chest feels uncomfortable, you feel numbness and tingling, and you have thoughts of death. Sound like fun? Hardly, but this may be a typical panic attack for people with *panic disorder*. Other symptoms could include: dizziness, abdominal discomfort, nausea, sweating, choking, flushing, feeling trapped, and fears of going crazy or out of control. These attacks often happen for no apparent reason. Sometimes the attacks are so frightening that people develop a fear of going out of the house (called agoraphobia) because they worry that they might have an attack while out. Panic attacks, like the other disorders we will discuss, can be very treatable with counseling and/or medication (often the combination is most appropriate).

Phobias are exaggerated fears of a specific object or situation. Examples of phobias include claustrophobia (fear of closed spaces), fear of high places, and fear of flying. These problems are often improved with a short bit of counseling. However, if you have a fear of flying and take only one plane trip per year, it may be helpful to take an anti-anxiety medication at the beginning of the flight.

People with *obsessive compulsive disorder* or *OCD* are bothered and even disabled by their obsessions and compulsions. Obsessions are recurrent or persistent thoughts that become intrusive. People with these disorders are so disturbed by these thoughts or ideas that they may feel compelled to do certain actions. For instance, they may have recurrent thoughts of being contaminated, compelling them to wash their hands excessively (perhaps even hundreds of times a day). Other obsessions may involve feelings of aggression or of losing control. We have all double checked that a door is locked or that the stove was turned off. However, with OCD this checking behavior may be excessive. This condition may also be improved with medication and behavioral counseling.

Generalized anxiety disorder refers to excessive anxiety throughout the day as opposed to the intermittent nature of the anxiety with panic disorder. *Social phobia* is a persistent fear of certain social situations. This might include an immobilizing fear of talking in front of others or having trouble eating in front of others.

Post-traumatic stress disorder (PTSD) became well known after the Vietnam War. This disorder occurs following a traumatic event that is outside the range of normal human experience. Traumatic events might include war experiences or other violent episodes, such as being raped or witnessing a murder. People with this problem have recurring or intrusive recollections of the event. They may have recurrent disturbing dreams and may be startled easily.

In addition to anxiety disorders, a common medical problem is *clinical depression*. This is different from occasionally being down or "depressed." With this disorder, the depressed mood occurs very frequently, for at least two weeks. Activities that formerly brought enjoyment cease to do so or they are abandoned entirely. With a clinical depression, there is often a change in appetite, weight loss or gain, fatigue and decreased concentration. Other common symptoms associated with depression are insomnia (especially early morning awakening with trouble getting back to sleep), trouble concentrating, feelings of worthlessness, excessive guilt, and recurrent thoughts of death.

If you have recurrent thoughts of suicide or if anyone you know starts talking about suicide, immediately seek professional attention.

Do not ignore these statements. If you do not know of a professional to call, call telephone information (411) for a suicide hotline or call 911. Pay attention if someone starts saying good-byes or starts giving away prized possessions. Part of the illness of clinical depression may include feelings of hopelessness and thoughts of never improving. Although depressed people often feel as if their conditions will never improve, the vast majority do improve, given time and the appropriate treatments. Suicide is in a sense a permanent solution to a temporary problem.

Both environmental and genetic factors contribute to anxiety disorders and depression. Why are some people more likely than others to develop a depression with a given stressful problem? One study found that people who had a variation in one particular gene were indeed more likely to develop depression with a given stressful life event.[44]

Seasonal Affective Disorder, or *SAD,* denotes depression that is prominent in the winter months. This disorder may respond to specifically-designed lights. Not infrequently, women may experience increased sadness or anxiety after having a baby. This is termed *post-partum depression* and may be caused by both the dramatic hormonal shifts and social changes that occur after delivering a baby. Post-partum depression is a temporary condition and usually responds to support groups, counseling and/or medication.* *Premenstrual syndrome (PMS)* designates excessive anxiety, depression, and possibly other symptoms such as breast swelling in the days preceding a woman's period. PMS responds to regular exercise and good nutrition, but for more severe cases medications such as antidepressants are very useful. *Dysthymia* is a low grade depression and the best treatment for it is somewhat controversial. The treatment might include counseling, antidepressants or even an herbal preparation called hypericum (St. John's Wort).**

Bipolar disorder (or manic depressive illness) is a condition where feelings of depression alternate with "manic" states. (Symptoms of mania

---

*As mentioned earlier, thyroid disorders are also not uncommon after delivery and are readily treatable if identified. They may also cause depression and/or anxiety.

**It is best to consult with your health care provider before starting this or certain other herbal products. Many herbal products, such as hypericum, have potential side effects and significant drug interactions.

may include elation, irritability, racing thoughts, increased energy, staying up all night, grandiosity, pressured speech, and irrational activity).

A disorder that has received recent recognition is *adult attention deficit disorder*. Attention deficit disorder (ADD) first appears in children who have trouble concentrating in class. Some, but not all of these children, are "hyperactive." When children with ADD become adults, their symptoms may or may not continue. Adults with ADD may have trouble concentrating and staying focused on a task.

If you believe that you, or someone you know, may have one of these disorders, discuss the issue with a health professional. Appropriate professionals might include your family doctor, internist, or psychiatrist. Counselors, psychologists or other qualilified therapists may also be helpful, but if medications are needed, you will need to talk with a medical doctor.

Daniel participated in my stress management class after seeing it advertised in a brochure. While in the class, he made quite a bit of progress with his stress. As he reviewed the class notes, he recognized that for many years he had experienced several of the symptoms associated with a clinical depression. He frequently suffered from fatigue, insomnia, decreased sex drive, and a variety of vague physical complaints. He had trouble concentrating and frequently felt sad. He realized that these symptoms had been present to one extent or another for many years. Although the techniques he learned in the class helped, he still felt sad much of the time.

For some reason, Daniel had previously seen this sadness as a sign of weakness. Even upon learning about the medical syndrome of depression, he was reluctant to seek treatment. Finally, he decided that life was too short to not do what he could to feel better. He went to see his family doctor who recommended that he start both an antidepressant medication and counseling. Daniel was not having much improvement after six weeks on the antidepressant. *His doctor however, was not discouraged, since he knew that there were perhaps 20 antidepressants on the market.*

Daniel was switched to another antidepressant and, after being on the treatment for approximately one month, he noticed a dramatic change in how he felt. The fatigue, insomnia, loss of sex drive, sadness, poor concentration, and physical symptoms were all improved. He finally felt like himself again and wondered why he had waited so long to seek treatment.

Dora was 61 years of age and had had a problem with anxiety since the fourth grade; she had started having panic attacks at the age of twelve. She had been through multiple medications and had seen many psychiatrists and counselors. She experienced some relief with the relaxation techniques that she had learned, along with a relatively small dose of alprazolam (a valium-type medication). Still, she was so bothered by panic attacks and agoraphobia that she would not drive.

In general, doctors avoid using too much of the benzodiazepine class of medication (valium-type drugs), since they are potentially addictive. However, if used carefully, they can be very beneficial. (Sometimes we use the benzodiazepines temporarily as we wait for the non-addictive medications to "kick in.") In Dora's case, I felt she was not getting adequate medication. I increased the total dose of alprazolam, but changed to an extended-release product which gave her more consistent relief. At the same time, I started her on a new antidepressant that should be effective for anxiety after it had some time to kick in.

I saw Dora two weeks later and she was amazed. She felt the best she "had felt in a **long** *time." She was peaceful* *throughout the day and could sleep at night. She felt "in control" and "ready to venture out." Putting it simply, she said, "I just feel good." This woman, who had suffered with a severe anxiety disorder for half a century, finally felt well. Prior to starting on the new medications, she said she was "at the end of her rope" and had even thought about suicide.*

Sometimes a person's biochemical abnormality is too great for counseling or stress management techniques alone. Dora's message to others was, "If you need help with medication, by all means, get help. If the first medicine does not work, don't be discouraged. Keep trying until you find something that does work."

Do not get me wrong; I am not a "pills-for-everyone doctor." The vast majority of people do very well without anxiety medication. However, some people do need it, and for those people, we need to remove any stigma associated with these medications. If you have high blood pressure and it is not controlled with diet and exercise, take medication before you have a heart attack or stroke. If you have clinical depression or an anxiety disorder and do not get adequate relief with stress management techniques and counseling, seek further help.

---

[43] Michels R., Marzuk P.M., "Progress in Psychiatry," *New England Journal of Medicine*, 1993; 13(II): 11–18.

[44] Caspi A., et al. "Influence of Life Stress on Depression: Moderation by a Polymorphism in the 5-HTT Gene." Science 2003; July 5; 327: 28–29.

15

Conclusion

Education is not the filling of a pail,
but the lighting of a fire.

WILLIAM BUTLER YEATS

I n this book, I have revealed a number of techniques that can be used to manage the stress in our lives. By reading this book and practicing the techniques that I have suggested, you are taking an active role in acquiring a happier and healthier life for yourself and for those around you.

Whatever stressful events you may encounter throughout your life, remember the importance of bringing yourself back to the present moment. Enjoy your life and those around you. Enjoy the next breath and feel the ground with each step. You do not need to clear your mind to have peace of mind, just enjoy that very next moment and pay keen attention to each sensation. Enjoy breathing, walking, eating, driving, showering, washing the dishes, and petting your dog.

Stress management is a lifelong practice. We frequently need to be reminded of stress management techniques. In that light, I encourage you to review selected chapters in this book and the CDs as needed. Additionally, utilize the reading list that follows to further explore stress management techniques.

At the end of a meditation, some people say a Loving Kindness prayer. This prayer takes on different forms. One form is say to yourself, "May I have peace and happiness, may my friends and family have peace and happiness, and may all people (or living beings) have peace and happiness." This wish sets a compassionate tone for the rest of your day following your meditation. At the end of a meditation, you might also imagine a scene that brings forth compassion, such as rocking a baby to sleep in your arms.

At the end of this book, this is also my wish for you:

> *May you have peace and happiness,*
> *and may your friends, family, and all of us*
> *have peace and happiness.*

CRCRD

Suggested Reading List

■ *General Stress Management and Health*

The Healthy Mind, Healthy Body Handbook by David S. Sobel, M.D. and Robert Ornstein, Ph.D. Los Altos: DRx, 1996.

The Wellness Book: The Comprehensive Guide to Maintaining Health and Treating Stress-Related Illness by Herbert Benson, M.D. and Eileen M. Stuart, R.N., C., M.S.; New York: Simon and Schuster, 1992.

Less Stress in 30 Days by Peggy R. Gillespie; New York: NAL/Dutton, 1987.

Healthy Pleasures by Robert Ornstein, Ph.D. and David Sobel, M.D.; New York: Addison-Wesley, 1989.

Don't Sweat the Small Stuff by Richard Carlson, Ph.D.; New York: Hyperion, 1997.

Minding the Body, Mending the Mind by Joan Borysenko, Ph.D., New York: Bantam Books, 1987.

Stressed is Desserts Spelled Backward by Brian Luke Seaward, Ph.D., Berkeley: Conari Press, 1999.

■ *General Stress Management Emphasizing Review of Research*

Mind Body Medicine edited by Daniel Goleman, Ph.D. and Joel Gurin, Yonkers: Consumer Reports Books, 1993.

Mind/Body Health; The Effects of Attitudes, Emotions, and Relationships by Brent Q. Hafen, Keith J. Karren, Kathryn J. Frandsen, and N. Lee Smith; Boston: Allyn & Bacon, 1996.

■ *Mindfulness*

Peace is Every Step by Thich Nhat Hahn; New York: Bantam Books, 1991.

Full Catastrophe Living by Jon Kabat-Zinn; New York: Dell Publishing, 1990.

Wherever You Go There You Are; Mindfulness Meditation in Everyday Life by Jon Kabat-Zinn; New York: Hyperion, 1994.

■ *Cognitive Therapy*

Feeling Good by David Burns, M.D., New York: Avon Books, 1980.

■ *Type A Personality*

Treating Type A Behavior and Your Heart by Meyer Friedman, M.D. and Diane Ulmer, R.N., M.S., New York: Ballantine Books, 1984.

■ *Lifestyle*

Simplify Your Life by Elaine St. James, New York: Hyperion, 1994.

Margin and *The Overload Syndrome* (these books are available together, in quite small print, or individually) by Richard Swenson, M.D., Colorado Springs, CO: Navpress, 2002.

■ *Communication*

Messages: The Communication Skills Book by Matthew McKay, Ph.D., Martha Davis, Ph.D., and Patrick Fanning, Oakland, CA: New Harbinger Publication, Inc., 1995.

How to Talk So Kids Will Listen & Listen So Kids Will Talk by Adele Faber and Elaine Mazlish, New York: Avon Books, 1980.

■ *Work-Related Stress*

Don't Sweat the Small Stuff at Work by Richard Carlson, Ph.D., New York: Hyperion, 1998.

The Truth About Burnout by Christina Maslach and Michael P. Leiter, San Francisco: Jossey-Bass Inc., Publishers, 1997.

■ *Relationships and Stress*

Don't Sweat the Small Stuff with Your Family by Richard Carlson, Ph.D., New York: Hyperion, 1998.

Love and Survival by Dean Ornish, M.D., New York: Harper Collins Publishers, 1998.

■ *Motivation*

Get the Edge by Anthony Robbins, San Diego: Robbins Research International, Inc., 2000 (available at www.gettheedge.com) (I have some disagreements with the energy/physiology section, but overall this is a very motivational product.)

■ *Anxiety Disorders*

The Anxiety Book by Jonathan Davidson, M.D. and Henry Dreher, New York: Penguin Putnam, 2003.

■ *Panic Disorder*

Don't Panic by R. Reid Wilson Ph.D., New York: Harper Collins Publishers, 1996.

■ *Depression*

Understanding Depression by Raymond J. DePaulo, M.D. and Leslie Ann Horvitz, John Wiley and Sons, 2002.

Tape Contents

Notes

Notes

Notes

Notes

ABOUT THE AUTHOR

Dr. Winner grew up in Baltimore, Maryland and obtained both his undergraduate and medical degrees at the University of Maryland. He completed a three-year residency in family practice at Franklin Square Hospital in Baltimore, where he also served as Chief Resident. Throughout his training, he maintained a strong interest in the field of stress management.

After residency, he enjoyed one year of traveling around the country and working as a family doctor. In 1991, he settled in Santa Barbara, where he continues his busy family practice. Since 1992, he has been teaching his popular stress management classes for the largest medical group in Santa Barbara, CA. In addition to teaching his courses for the general public, he has conducted seminars and workshops for numerous groups including medical offices, government employees and a variety of businesses.

As both a family physician and a teacher of stress management, Dr. Winner has a deep appreciation for both the physical and psychological effects of stress. He has helped thousands of people deal with stress-related problems.

He resides in Santa Barbara with his wife and his two-year-old twin sons.

For comments, suggestions or stories
of how you or someone else successfully
managed your stress: please contact us at
comments@stressremedy.com. We appreciate any feedback.
Unfortunately, we are unable to answer questions via email.

Give the gift of better health
to your friends and colleagues.

☐ Please send _____ copies of *Stress Management Made Simple* for $34.95 each.

My check or money order for $_____ is enclosed.

■ For faster service, go to ***www.stressremedy.com.***

Name _____

Organization _____

Address _____

City/State/Zip _____

Email _____

Phone_____

**Include $4.95 shipping and handling for the first book
and $1.00 for each additional book.**

California residents please add 7.75% sales tax.

*Payment must accompany all orders.
Allow 3 weeks for delivery.*

Please send to:
Blue Fountain Press
Suite 104
2026 Cliff Drive
Santa Barbara, CA 93109

www.stressremedy.com

Give the gift of better health
to your friends and colleagues.

☐ Please send _____ copies of *Stress Management Made Simple* for
$34.95 each.

My check or money order for $_____ is enclosed.

■ For faster service, go to ***www.stressremedy.com.***

Name _____

Organization _____

Address _____

City/State/Zip _____

Email _____

Phone_____

**Include $4.95 shipping and handling for the first book
and $1.00 for each additional book.**

California residents please add 7.75% sales tax.

Payment must accompany all orders.
Allow 3 weeks for delivery.

Please send to:
Blue Fountain Press
Suite 104
2026 Cliff Drive
Santa Barbara, CA 93109

www.stressremedy.com